# sew & stitch
# embroidery

## 20+ SIMPLE SEWING PROJECTS WITH
## 30+ FRESH HAND EMBROIDERY DESIGNS

## by Alyssa Thomas

## Photography by Sarah Hebenstreit

D&C
David and Charles

# Contents

# Introduction

I was first introduced to embroidery when I was five or six years old. My parents left for the evening, and my babysitter brought over a cross-stitch project she was working on. I was glued to her the entire evening. I watched her stitch, one "X" after another, fascinated and anxiously waiting to see the finished design. The next day, I had my mom take me down to our local craft store to buy a cross-stitch kit of my very own. I went on to cross-stitch and embroider my fair share of Christmas ornaments and wildlife animals.

I love to embroider. I love that by tracing a line with a row of simple stitches you can create a piece of art, full of color and texture. I love seeing a design come to life on fabric, and it's rewarding to know that it's something I've made myself.

I'm a firm believer that embroidery can be more than an embellishment. Embroidery can be bold and attention getting. In this book you'll find projects in which embroidery is the star, like in the "What a Lovely Evening" Owl Wall Art, Octopus Quilt, Dream Catcher, and Outer Space Parachute for your favorite toy. Throughout the book, you'll find opportunities to stitch the quirky characters from my design company, Penguin & Fish. Create sweet owls, a tiny hedgehog, a giant octopus, a racing elephant, and even a couple dinosaurs—all embroidered and sewn into exciting projects for the home, to wear, to play with and to carry and use.

One of my favorite things to do with embroidery is to enlarge the designs and stitch them really big. For several projects, we'll supersize our embroidery hoop by exchanging it for a quilting hoop and instead of floss we'll use yarn to make these "big stitches."

I've designed the projects in this book to excite you rather than intimidate you. That said, to complete most of them, you do need basic working knowledge of a sewing machine and how to sew a straight stitch. I've included a Sewing Skill Level with each project: Level 1 involves zero sewing, so anyone can do it! Level 2 is for sewing beginners and uses primarily straight stitching and only a few steps. Level 3 can also be completed by a beginner but involves more steps and more complicated skills, such as adding zippers. I've also included an Embroidery Skill Level for each project to help you determine which designs are best suited to you.

Now grab a needle, hoop and floss, and let's get started.

**Happy stitching!**

# Embroidery Essentials

## TOOLS, MATERIALS, STITCHES AND MORE

Embroidery is a fantastic craft for so many reasons: It's relaxing, portable, simple to do and cheap. To get started, all you need is a needle, embroidery floss, an embroidery hoop and fabric. All are inexpensive and pretty easy to find. After you learn a stitch or two, all you need to do is trace over a line with stitches or fill in a shape like a coloring book. Easy! In this section, you will see the basic tools and materials for embroidery and find out how to use them. The stitch library on pages 20–25 shows all the stitches you need to know to complete an embroidered design. You'll also get simple machine-sewing techniques that will help you create the projects in the book. And all along the way, I'll share some tips and tricks that will help you stitch your very best.

# Tools and Materials

To begin embroidering, the only tools you really need are a needle, an embroidery hoop and scissors. All of these are inexpensive and available at your local craft store. Below is a list of basic embroidery tools (tools for stitching both standard and large embroideries) and other helpful embroidery tools, as well as sewing and crafting tools.

# For Stitching: Embroidery Tools

## For Standard Embroidery
By "standard" embroidery, I am referring to the small, traditional embroidery stitches, not the large stitches you would use on large projects (see below).

**Embroidery needle:** A hand sewing needle with a sharp point and a long eye to fit strands of embroidery floss.

**Embroidery hoop:** A wood or plastic hoop used to hold fabric while embroidering. Each hoop is sized by the hoop diameter (e.g., 8" or 10") and has an inner ring, outer ring and a closure to secure the hoops and fabric in place.

**Embroidery scissors:** A small, high-quality pair of scissors with a sharp point.

## For Large Embroidery

**Chenille needle:** A large-eye needle with a sharp tip. The large eye allows thicker yarn to fit through. Choose a chenille needle when you are using yarn and big stitches.

**Tapestry needle:** Similar to a chenille needle but with a blunt tip. The blunt tip allows it to pass through loosely woven fabric, like burlap, without piercing the fibers.

**Quilting hoop:** A wood or plastic hoop used to secure fabric for hand-stitching quilts or for large embroidery projects. Quilting hoops are typically larger then embroidery hoops. The hoop I like to use has a 24" diameter.

### Basic Embroidery Kit
In most of the projects, you will see Basic Embroidery Kit listed in the Supplies section. The kit includes:
    embroidery needle*
    embroidery hoop*
    water-soluble marker (or other transfer materials such as iron-on transfer paper)
    embroidery scissors
    iron and ironing board
*If the project specifies "for big stitches," you will need a chenille needle in place of an embroidery needle and a quilting hoop in place of an embroidery hoop.

**Standard Embroidery**
six-strand embroidery floss, embroidery needle, embroidery hoops

**Sewing**
fabric scissors, rotary cutter, thread

**Floss and Yarn**
floss, worsted-weight yarn

# For Transferring

**Iron-on transfer pattern:** Manufactured patterns printed in reverse with heat-transferable ink. When you lay the transfer paper image-side down and press a hot iron over it, the image appears correctly. Be sure not to confuse this with printable T-shirt iron-on transfer paper, which is a different product and will leave a plastic residue on your fabric surface.

**Carbon transfer paper:** Carbon paper (and also graphite paper) is a reusable paper with a thin layer of carbon (or graphite). Carbon paper comes in several colors, even white, so you can use it on dark fabrics.

**Water-soluble markers:** A wash-away marker used to transfer your motif.

**Heat-sensitive pens:** My new favorite tool! Heat-sensitive pens, such as the FriXion pens by Pilot, write like standard ink pens, but have heat-sensitive ink. Use them to transfer motifs to fabric; then, when your embroidering is finished, run a hot iron over them to make the ink disappear. The pens do leave a transparent residue, so it's important to mark only areas that are going to be stitched. Also, if the ink gets cold, like if you would take a quilt outside in cold weather, the ink comes back and needs to be ironed again to make it disappear. If you're working on an heirloom-quality embroidery, I wouldn't recommend using the heat-sensitive pen, because it hasn't been tested to see if it damages fabric over time. However, for your everyday embroidery and quilting needs, this kind of pen is awesome! Check out your local office-supply store to find heat-sensitive pens.

**Iron-on transfer pen or pencil:** A pen or pencil containing iron-on ink (or other materials) that when ironed will transfer a design to fabric. Sulky iron-on transfer pens are my favorite; they come in lots of different colors, even white to use on dark fabrics. These can typically be found at online retailers.

**Embroidery stabilizers:** Stabilizers are typically used for machine embroidery. They attach to the back of fabric to keep it from stretching during the sewing process. You would use stablizers on the front of fabric as an embroidery transfer tool. There are four basic types of stabilizers, and they relate to how you remove the stabilizer when you're done embroidering: cut-away (or permanent), tear-away, heat-away and water-soluble. There are also different types of ways they can be attached to fabric, including sew-in, stick-on, and fusible or iron-on. It's important to get the right combination of "putting on" and "taking off." For most projects, I recommend using tear-away fusible embroidery stabilizer, such as Pellon's Fuse-N-Tear and Sulky's Totally Stable, or the stick-on water soluable type, such as Sulky's Sticky Fabri-Solvy.

# For Fun

**Embroidery stand:** A stand that props up your embroidery for you so you don't always have to have a hoop in your hand. They can come in floor or lap versions. They're certainly not necessary to get the job done, but might make your job more fun.

**Movie:** Embroidery is super relaxing to do while you watch a fun movie. I would recommend *Dirty Dancing* or the *Back to the Future* trilogy.

# For Sewing: Tools

**Sewing machine:** You'll need a machine that can do a straight stitch and a backstitch (back tack), which most do, as well as other types of stitches. There are lots of machines to choose from, so just be sure to use one that you are comfortable with. You don't need a fancy, complicated machine to complete the projects in this book.

**Zipper foot:** A sewing machine presser foot meant for the purpose of sewing on zippers.

**Iron and ironing board:** Essential tools for preparing your embroidery (transferring motifs and ironing out wrinkles) and completing sewing projects (ironing seams flat, keeping folds in place). Keep in mind that ironing is referred to as "pressing" when sewing.

**Fabric scissors:** A sharp, high-quality pair of scissors for cutting fabric and yarn.

**Pinking shears:** A sharp, high-quality pair of scissors with a zigzagged edge for cutting fabric. The zigzagged edge helps keep fabric from fraying.

**Rotary cutter:** A circular blade attached to a handle. It's used for cutting fabric and is most commonly used with a self-healing cutting mat and a quilting grid ruler.

**Self-healing cutting mat:** A plastic mat with a measuring grid. It's used to protect table surfaces while cutting fabric with a rotary cutter.

**Quilting grid rulers:** Clear plastic rulers with a grid used for precise measuring and cutting of fabric with a rotary cutter and self-healing cutting mat.

**Pin cushion and pins:** Long pins used to hold your pieces of fabric together for sewing. A pin cushion keeps your pins in one place and prevents them from spilling. Magnetic pin cushions are my favorite.

**Bent-arm safety pins:** Bent-arm safety pins look like normal safety pins, except they have a bend in the middle. They are used to temporarily baste the layers of a quilt together before hand- or machine-quilting.

**Seam ripper:** A seam ripper is a tool used to cut open a seam. You're less likely to accidentally cut your fabric when using a seam ripper over a pair of scissors.

**Fabric glue:** A glue to permanently hold together two pieces of fabric.

**Glue gun:** An electric gun that puts out beads of hot glue for fusing items together.

**Chopstick:** A great tool not only for eating sushi, but also for pushing out corners and placing stuffing in toys.

## Basic Sewing Kit
In several of the projects, you will see Basic Sewing Kit listed in the Supplies section. The kit includes:
- sewing machine
- pins
- sewing scissors
- matching thread
- iron and ironing board

# For Sewing: Fabric and Notions

Below is a helpful guide to knowing and picking your materials. Choosing the right fabric for the job is the starting point for all of the embroidery projects in this book.

## Know Your Fabric

**Quilt-weight cotton:** Most of the projects made using small stitches with floss (basic embroidery) call for high-quality, quilt-weight cotton fabric. Quilt-weight cotton is a tightly woven fabric with vertical and horizontal grain lines. I recommend choosing a light-colored, solid quilt-weight fabric for embroidery, as that fabric will allow the stitches to stand out best. To add color, you can choose patterned quilt-weight cotton for linings, backings and other areas without embroidery.

**A fat quarter** is a common cut of quilt-weight cotton and refers to a yard of fabric that has been cut once in half lengthwise and again crosswise. A fat quarter typically measures 18" x 22" (46cm x 56cm).

**Linen:** Linen is best for projects using big embroidery stitches. Linen is a woven fabric that is made from flax. It has a lovely texture, and its loose weave can accommodate larger stitches made with yarn better than quilt-weight cotton fabric. Linen is prone to wrinkling, so it's important to take your embroidery out of the hoop when you're not working on it to avoid putting permanent creases in the fabric.

**Cotton flannel:** Cotton flannel is a woven fabric that has a brushed surface (nap) on one or both sides to add extra softness. The soft nap allows two pieces of cotton flannel to "stick" together.

### Knowing the Width of Your Fabric
In shops, fabric is stored on cardboard rolls called bolts. On quilt-weight cotton, it's typical that fabric is 42" (107cm) wide, folded in half, then rolled into a bolt. Other fabrics like linen and burlap may be wider then 42" (107cm) but sometimes less. Many home decorating fabrics come in widths much larger than 42" (107cm). It's important to check how wide the fabric is to ensure you buy the right amount, especially before cutting it.

### Anatomy of Woven Fabric

**Selvage:** The tightly woven edge on either side of a width of fabric.

**Grain:** The direction of the woven fibers that run the length and width of the fabric. Lengthwise grain runs parallel to the selvage. It is the strongest grain in a woven fabric. Crosswise grain runs perpendicular to the selvages and is slightly stretchier.

**Bias:** The diagonal grain of the fabric. This is the stretchiest part of woven fabric.

**Right side versus wrong side:** The right side of fabric is the side where the pattern is printed, and the wrong side is the opposite. Many solid colored fabrics have no visible right or wrong side. When embroidered, the wrong side refers to the back of the embroidery.

**Burlap:** Burlap is a coarse and loosely woven fabric made from jute or hemp. I like to use it as a decorative cloth with a lot of texture and character. It also works well for big stitches and yarn because of its loose weave.

**Wool felt:** Instead of its fibers lining up vertically and horizontally like woven fabric, wool felt's fibers go in every direction and are matted together. This means you can cut shapes out and the edges won't fray.

**Cross-stitch fabric:** Cross-stitch fabric is woven evenly with a set thread count per inch. The threads create small squares that form an easily countable grid. Cross-stitch fabric comes in a variety of numbered sizes, representing squares per inch.

## Notions and Other Materials

**Batting (or Wadding):** Batting is the layer on the inside of a quilt that gives the quilt its fluffiness and warmth. It comes in sheet form in different thicknesses or lofts (low loft is thin, high loft is thick) and can be made of wool, cotton, polyester, bamboo and even recycled plastic bottles.

**Stuffing:** Stuffing is the loose fluffy fiber used to stuff toys. I use polyester fiberfill because it's lightweight, machine washable and easy to find. Other stuffings available include wool, cotton and bamboo.

**Double-sided iron-on adhesive:** Double-sided iron-on adhesive is used to fuse two pieces of fabric and comes in sheet form. Peel the paper on one side of the adhesive and iron it to the back side of your fabric. Then remove the other side of paper and iron to your second fabric. (Getting the fusible heat-bond adhesive directly onto your iron could damage your iron.)

**Interfacing:** Interfacings are used to give sturdiness and heft to fabric. They come in different weights and can be sewn in or ironed-on (called fusible). I use either a medium-weight or heavy-weight interfacing when I'm making a bag to give it a boxier appearance.

**Other notions:** You may need a few other other materials on hand, depending on the needs of the project. For example, zippers and buttons will give you options for bag closures, and ribbons make a nice, decorative drawstring. D-rings (metal rings in the shape of the letter "D") will allow you to attach a removable strap to a clutch, while pin backs help you turn a simple piece of felt into a lovely brooch.

# For Stitching: Floss and Yarn

**Six-strand embroidery floss:** Embroidery floss is a loosely twisted thread that comes in six strands. The strands are typically separated into fewer strands to achieve different line weights. For the projects in this book, you need to separate the strands in half and use three strands in the embroideries. Embroidery floss is manufactured by several companies and comes in hundreds of colors and styles. For the projects here, you will use the most common style of floss: the six-strand mercerized cotton floss. Mercerized cotton refers to the process the cotton floss goes through to give the cotton strength, luster and the ability to better hold on to dye. Feel free to experiment with other styles of floss like metallic, satin or even glow-in-the-dark floss!

**Perle (or Pearl) cotton floss:** Perle cotton is a decorative floss made of two tightly twisted strands that cannot be separated easily. Perle cotton is great for blanket stitching an edge and works well for hand quilting because it is typically stronger then embroidery floss, and its twisted strands give it a decorative touch.

**Yarn:** Yarn is a long length of twisted fibers and is used for all sorts of crafts including knitting, crochet and weaving. It's used to create the embroideries for the larger projects in this book. Yarn comes in many weights and fibers. I used mainly a worsted weight yarn which is a common, medium thickness yarn. I pick yarns mostly for their color and size rather than for their fiber. For projects that need special care—for example, if you plan to wash the project at some point—make sure to read the care instructions on the yarn to make sure the yarn works with how you'd like to use it.

# Embroidery Techniques

Now that you have your tools and materials, it's time to start embroidering! Below is all the info, tips and tricks you need to get it done: how to transfer and enlarge your design, get started stitching, and find the essential stitch library, plus see simple sewing techniques for making lovely projects from what you stitch.

## Transferring the Pattern

The first step to embroidery is getting your design onto your fabric. This can be accomplished in several different ways depending on personal preference and the type of fabric you're transferring your design to. Below are several ways to transfer your design to fabric.

## Transferring to Standard Fabric

By "standard" fabric, I mean nonstretchy, nonsquishy fabric, such as quilt-weight cotton, linen or flannel.

### Tracing Onto Fabric

This is my favorite and the most basic technique for transferring designs to fabric. It works best for light-colored fabrics, nonstretchy fabrics and a simple designs. Use a water-soluble marker or heat-sensitive pen to ensure your transfer marks will not be permanent.

#### HOW TO TAPE TO A SUNNY WINDOW

1 Simple! Tape your embroidery pattern to a bright window. Tape your fabric to the window on top of the pattern. Try not to stretch the fabric as you secure it. You should be able to see the pattern behind the fabric. Trace the pattern using a water soluble marker, heat-sensitive pen or sharp pencil.

#### HOW TO USE A LIGHT TABLE OR BOX

2 In lieu of a window, you can use a light table or box. A light table is a table or flat box with a glass top and a light that shines from underneath glass. Light tables are available at most craft stores. The steps are the same as for using a sunny window.

## Manufactured Iron-On Transfer

An iron-on transfer is a design that is commercially printed onto paper using a heat-sensitive ink. It is printed in reverse, and once it is transferred to fabric, it appears in the correct direction. Ink is permanent or semipermanent, and the transfer can be used about five times. I give this method two thumbs up for speed and ease, especially if you're transferring an intricate design. But don't use an iron-on transfer if you're worried about the permanence of the lines. Keep in mind that in most cases, your embroidery stitches will cover up the lines. The biggest drawback to iron-on transfers is that they're not always available. There are companies that are starting to carry their designs in iron-on transfer (including Penguin & Fish); however, that doesn't help if you're drawing your own image or if you downloaded a PDF design from a Web site. If you do have an iron-on transfer, I'd say use it. You'll get to embroidering much faster!

The pull-out Transfer Sheet at the back of the book contains patterns for several of the projects in the book. The Transfer Sheet is a manufactured iron-on transfer.

## HOW TO USE THE IRON-ON TRANSFER

Set your iron to "no steam." It's a good idea to place some paper on the ironing board under the fabric to protect the ironing board in case the transfer goes through the fabric onto the board. Preheat your fabric by ironing it for a few seconds.

Place the iron-on transfer on top of the fabric with the transfer facing down against the fabric. Hold the iron on top of the transfer for about 10 seconds. Lift the iron up to press another section of the transfer. Try to avoid moving the iron around on top of the transfer because the transfer will move slightly and make your transfer blurry. Peek to see if the design transferred all the way, and then remove transfer.

### Make Your Own Iron-On Transfer

You can make your own iron-on transfer using an iron-on transfer pen or pencil. You can use the transfer several times, but keep in mind that, as with manufactured iron-on transfers, the lines are permanent. Although this method is very easy, the pen's lines can be a little thick, so I prefer using one of the tracing methods that give me lines that disappear when I'm done embroidering.

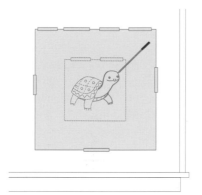

## HOW TO MAKE YOUR OWN
## IRON-ON TRANSFER

Make sure to start with a reversed or mirrored version of your design. Place a heavy piece of tracing paper or vellum over the pattern. Using the iron-on transfer pen, trace over the design. You can also draw directly onto

your patterns; however, if you'd like to use it again in the future, it's best to trace the design to the tracing paper. Transfer the design to your fabric in the same way you would a commerical iron-on transfer (see above).

### Carbon (or Graphite) Transfer Paper

Using carbon (or graphite) transfer paper is another simple way to transfer your motif to fabric. It's reusable and removable and a great option for transferring homemade motifs or designs from PDF patterns downloaded from the Internet. And it's my go-to technique when a fabric is too difficult to trace through. One drawback of carbon transfer paper is that sometimes, after transferring the motif to fabric, the motif can rub off before finishing. After transferring the motif, it's helpful to go over the lines quickly with a water-soluble marker or heat-sensitive pen.

## HOW TO USE CARBON
## TRANSFER PAPER

Place your fabric on a hard surface. Set the carbon transfer paper, carbon side down, on top of the fabric. Place your pattern on top of the carbon transfer paper (motif side up) and fabric and pin through all the layers to hold your motif in place. Using a dull pencil or metal stylus (or your grandma's tiny metal crochet hook like I use), trace the motif with a firm and even pressure. You may want to peek under the transfer paper to see if your motif is transferring properly. After you're finished, remove your pins, pattern, and carbon paper. If desired, trace over the lines quickly with a water-soluble marker or heat-sensitive pen.

### Transferring to Dark-Colored Fabric

The easiest way to transfer your motif onto a dark-colored fabric is with white or a light-colored carbon transfer paper. Follow the carbon transfer paper instructions (above). You can also use the embroidery stabilizer technique on page 16.

# Transferring to Specialty Fabric

By "specialty" fabric, I mean stretchy, squishy, loosely woven or thick fabrics such as knits, burlap and felt.

## Embroidery Stabilizer

When I'm working with a specialty fabric, I like to use an embroidery stabilizer for transferring the design. Most often, I use the fusible tear-away or stick-on water soluble types of stabilizer because they are simple to adhere to fabric. However, when I'm nervous about getting my fabric wet or heating it with an iron, I'll use sew-in tear-away stabilizer. Whatever kind you choose, the stabilizer will provide support while stitching, so you typically don't need to use an embroidery hoop to hold the fabric in place. However, if you're using a very thin fabric you may still want to use an embroidery hoop with your stabilizer for extra support.

### HOW TO TRANSFER THE DESIGN TO STABILIZER

Cut a piece of stabilizer that is at least 1" (2.5cm) bigger all the way around than your design. If you plan on using an embroidery hoop, make sure the stabilizer is at least 1" (2.5cm) larger then your hoop. With the fusible (or sticky) side down, place your stabilizer on top of your design and trace using a pen or pencil. You can also print your design directly onto the stabilizer. (Printing instructions should be included with your stabilizer.)

### HOW TO ADD AND REMOVE FUSIBLE, TEAR-AWAY STABILIZER

Preheat your fabric with the iron and then iron the stabilizer (with your design traced or printed on it) to the fabric. Then stitch your design through both the fabric and stabilizer. To remove the stabilizer when you're finished stitching, first tear away any large pieces. Then gently and carefully tear away the stabilizer around the edge of the stitches and around each individual stitch. If you accidentally loosen a stitch by pulling on it too much, tighten the stitch by pulling on it from the back of your embroidery.

### HOW TO ADD AND REMOVE STICK-ON WATER-SOLUBLE STABILIZER

After tracing on your design, remove the paper backing and stick the stabilizer to your fabric. Then stitch your design through both the fabric and stabilizer. To remove the stabilizer when you're finished stitching, submerge tha fabric in warm water and gently agitate with your hand for about three minutes. Rinse the fabric in cold water and let the fabric air dry.

### HOW TO ADD AND REMOVE SEW-IN TEAR-AWAY STABILIZER

After tracing on your design, using sewing thread, hand stitch the sew-in, tear-away stabilizer to your fabric with long basting stitches. Then stitch your design through both the fabric and stabilizer. To remove the stabilizer, cut away the basting stitches and then tear away any large pieces of stabilizer. Gently and carefully remove the stabilizer around the edge of the stitches and around each individual stitch. If you accidentally loosen a stitch by pulling on it too much, tighten the stitch by pulling on it from the back of your embroidery.

# Enlarging the Design

For some projects, you will need to make the design larger than it is printed on the pattern sheet. If your intended design size is smaller than a standard (letter-sized) sheet of paper, all you need to do is print or copy it at whatever enlargement you need (such as 200%). Other times, the actual design needs to be larger than a sheet of printer paper. In these cases, use one of the methods below for enlarging the design.

All the designs and templates in this book tell you how much to enlarge the design to make it the size needed for the project. If no enlargement is given, the design is the correct size.

## Tiled Photocopies or Printouts

### HOW TO MAKE TILED PRINTS

Set your photocopier or your print dialog box to the percentage you would like to enlarge your design. Photocopy or print until all parts of the design have been printed at the larger size. Tape the printouts together, and your pattern is ready to transfer.

## Large-Format KIP printer

Large format KIP printers or plotters are commonly used by architects to photocopy or print their blueprints. These printers can often be found at your local copy center. It's best to ask the copy center staff to help you use the KIP printer because they can be a little touchy. Also, don't let the copy center staff talk you into an expensive large print from one of their other banner printers. Prints from the KIP printer are usually less than five dollars.

## Grid Method

The grid method is an age-old, low-tech way of enlarging a design. It breaks up a design into smaller parts that are easier to draw. The grid method can be effective when you're making an especially large design like the Octopus quilt (page 24) The drawback is that it's time consuming and can take some practice.

### HOW TO USE THE GRID METHOD

I  Using a ruler and sharp pencil, draw lines on your pattern dividing the design in half lengthwise and widthwise. Continue to draw a grid of squares on top of the design with the squares ¾" (2cm) or 1" (2.5cm) in size.

2  Next, using a water-soluble marker, mark your fabric with lines dividing your fabric in half lengthwise and widthwise within the outer edge. Mark the outer edge of where you'd like your design to be.

3  On the pattern, count the number of grid squares from the center line to the edge. On your fabric, measure the distance from the center line to the edge. Divide that number by the number of squares on the pattern, from the center to the edge on the design. Draw lines on your fabric accordingly. Continue using the same measurement until you have a grid that matches the one of the pattern.

4  Number each square on the design starting in the upper left corner. Repeat with the squares on the fabric mimicking the numbers on the design.

5  Now it's time to start drawing. Pick any square on the design and start drawing the contents of that square in the coordinating square on the fabric using a water soluble marker. Pay especially close attention to where lines enter and exit the square. If a square is still too detailed to figure it out, divide the square on the design and fabric in half again and focus on the contents of the smaller squares.

6  Continue to draw until every square is finished. Step back from the fabric and look at the drawing often. Looking at the whole drawing will help you see if a line or arc is a little wonky and needs to be adjusted.

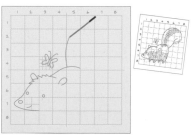

# Starting and Stopping Your Embroidery

## Preparing to Stitch

Every time you begin a project, first prepare to stitch by getting the hoop and floss ready.

### PLACE FABRIC INTO HOOP

Loosen the screw closure and separate the inner and outer hoops. Lay the inner hoop on a flat surface. Place your fabric on top of the inner hoop, making sure the fabric hangs over the inner hoop's edge by at least 1" (2.5cm) all the way around. Place the outer hoop on top of the fabric and press down over the inner hoop. Gently pull your fabric taut without separating the two hoops. Once your fabric is pulled evenly across the hoop, tighten the screw closure.

When you're finished stitching, take your embroidery out of the hoop. Leaving it in the hoop can permanently crease your fabric.

### PREPARE EMBROIDERY FLOSS

Refer to the appropriate pattern and stitch and color guide to determine where you will begin stitching and which color floss you need. Cut a piece of embroidery floss to about 24" (61cm). If you're using six-strand embroidery floss, divide the six strands in half to create two pieces of floss that have three strands each.

## Starting and Stopping the Stitches

How you begin and end a row of stitches is just as important as the stitches themselves.

## To Knot or Not?

Typically, to start the stitches of your embroidery, you bring your threaded needle from the back of your fabric through to the front and then start your first stitch. But how do you stop the end of your floss from slipping through? The simplest way is to just tie a knot at the end of the floss (which is what I often do). However, a knot on the back of the fabric can make a bump on the front of your embroidery that you don't want. Also, if you're embroidering something that will be washed, your knot can become untied. Two better options to secure the end of your floss involve making temporary knots.

### USING THE "AWAY KNOT"

1  Tie a knot at the end of your floss. Bring your needle through the front of the fabric to the back at least 5" (13cm) away from where you want to start stitching.

---

**Livin' Large: Stitching a Large-Scale Design**

Stitching a large embroidery is much the same as stitching a small embroidery. The only difference is that everything gets bigger. Instead of an embroidery hoop, use an 18" to 24" (46cm to 61cm) quilting hoop. Instead of embroidery floss, use a worsted weight yarn. Instead of an embroidery needle, use a chenille needle, which has a bigger eye that's large enough for yarn to be threaded through. Instead of using quilt-weight cotton fabric, use linen or a fabric with a looser weave. The looser weave will allow the yarn to pass through it more easily than quilt-weight cotton fabric. See the For Sewing: Fabric and Notions section (on page 12) for more information on the individual items. Also go to Enlarging a Design (on page 17) for instructions on how to enlarge and transfer your design to get it ready for your large embroidery project. You also get to make your embroidery stitches larger. Instead of a single stitch being ⅛" (3mm), you can make each stitch 1" to 2" (2.5cm to 5cm) Often this means that a large embroidery is quicker to finish than a small embroidery. Woo hoo!

---

**2** Bring your needle from the back of the fabric through the front where you would like to start your first stitch. Embroider your design until you reach the end of the floss. Finish stitching as needed (see The End of the Line below).

**3** Snip away your starting knot. Thread the tail of the floss through your needle and weave the end through the back of your stitches as you did with the other end of floss.

## USING THE "WASTE KNOT"

**I** Tie a knot at the end of your floss. Decide where your first line of stitches is going to be. Bring your needle through the front of the fabric to the back about 2" (5cm) along that line.

**2** Bring your needle from the back of the fabric through the front where you would like to start your first stitch. Start your embroidery. As you embroider toward your knot, make sure the backs of your stitches are going over the tail of your floss, securing the floss in place.

**3** Once you've secured the tail of the floss with several stitches, snip away the knot from the front of your embroidery. Continue with your embroidery.

# *The End of the Line*

No matter what stitches you use to complete a design, always end a peice of floss and the project in the same way.

## HIDE THE FLOSS END

When you get to the end of the floss, turn your work over and weave in the end through the backs of your stitches. Weave the tail of your floss back and forth at least once to lock it in place. Trim the tail close to the stitches.

## IRON YOUR EMBROIDERY

When you're finished with your embroidery, unscrew the closure on your hoop and take out your fabric. Iron around the edges where the embroidery was in the hoop and avoid ironing the actual embroidery if possible. If ironing the embroidery is necessary, first lay a plush towel on top of your ironing board and then place your embroidery facedown on top of the towel. This will help preserve your three-dimensional stitches while ironing. You don't want to flatten all of your pretty stitches!

## REMOVE PEN MARKS

Before moving on to the rest of a project, remove any marks left by the water soluble marker (or heat-senstive pen). If the rest of the project involves adding additional marks, you can wait until the end of the project before removing the marks.

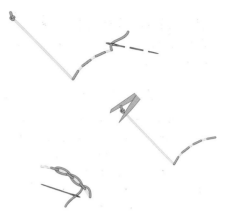

**Away Knot**

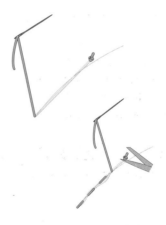

**Waste Knot**

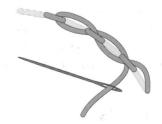

**Hide the floss end**

# Embroidery Stitch Library

There are many different individual and combinations of embroidery stitches. Personally, I like to keep my designs pretty simple and believe you can do a lot with just a few different embroidery stitches. In each project, you'll use a minimum of two different stitches to complete the embroidery motif. Once you get comfortable with your different embroidery stitches, feel free to use them in a project to make the embroidery your own. Instead of just outlining a shape, you might want to fill it in. If, for example, you like using a split stitch instead of a backstitch, feel free to change it. Below is a guide of beginning stitches that will get you off and running.

A Note About the Projects: Each motif includes a stitch and color guide, which tells you which stitches to use to complete the motif. It also suggests which colors to use for the stitches. You can find the stitch and color guides beginning on page 116.

## Stitches for Outlining

### Backstitch

The backstitch is my go-to stitch for outlining. It makes for a nice clean row of stitches.

**How to:** Start from the back of the fabric and bring the needle through. Make your first stitch by putting your needle through the front of the fabric in a backward direction from the direction you would like your line to go. Start the second stitch by bringing the needle back up through the fabric a stitch length away from your original starting point. Finish the second stitch by putting your needle through the original starting point.

**Backstitch**

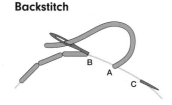

### Split stitch

I like the split stitch if I want a line to look a little more organic.

**How to:** Bring your needle up from the back of the fabric on the line you want to stitch and then make one stitch about ¼" (6mm) in length along the line. Bring the needle up and slightly back from where you inserted it, bringing it up directly through your last stitch, splitting the strands of floss. Continue stitching your line.

**Split stitch**

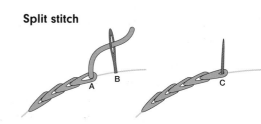

### Stem stitch

The stem stitch is a traditional embroidery stitch used for outlining. It's often used for the stems of flowers.

**How to:** Bring your needle through from the back of your fabric on the line you want to stitch. Make a stitch about ¼" (6mm) in length, inserting the needle slightly to the right of the line. Bring your needle back to the front, on the line and slightly back, so it's next to your previous stitch. For a thicker line, make your stitches smaller and increase the angle of the stitches. For a thinner line, lengthen your stitches and decrease the angle.

**Stem stitch**

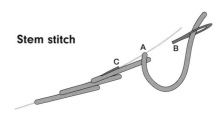

# Running stitch

The running stitch is often the first stitch learned by a beginner. It creates a cute dashed line.

**How to:** Bring your needle through from the back of the fabric on the line you want to stitch. Insert the needle about ⅛" (3mm) in length away along the line to create your first stitch. Bring your needle out from the back a stitch length away. Continue along the line. You can also weave your stitches in and out of the fabric to make several stitches at once.

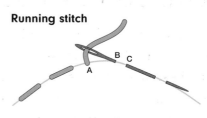

**Running stitch**

# Chain stitch

The chain stitch is made up of interlocking loops. It's one of my favorite stitches because it reminds me of a crocheted chain stitch. Stitch several rows right next to each other, and it makes a great stitch to fill in shapes!

**How to:** At your starting point, bring your needle up from the back of the fabric. Insert the needle back through the starting point. Next, bring the needle up through the fabric a stitch length away (about ⅛" ([3mm] in length). Pull your needle up through the loop, making the loop smaller in the process. Keep pulling until the loop meets the point where the floss exits the fabric. Repeat for the additional stitches in your row. To end your row, make a tiny stitch over your last loop, securing it in place (an anchoring stitch). To turn at a corner, make an anchoring stitch in the same way and then come back up again on the inside of your last loop. Start stitching in the new direction.

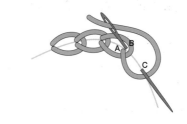

**Chain stitch**

# Stitches for Filling in Shapes

# Seed stitch

This easy stitch is my go-to stitch for a casual, speckled fill or for making animal hair.

**How to:** Bring your needle up from the back of the fabric. Insert the needle a short distance from the starting point. Continue with more stitches. Typically, seed stitches are stitched in all different directions, making a random pattern. However, if I'm stitching something like animal hair, I often make stitches that go in the same direction.

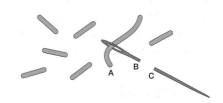

**Seed stitch**

# Satin stitch

The satin stitch is what I use most often to completely fill in a small space. If your space is bigger, it might be better to use the long and short stitch (below).

**How to:** Bring the needle up from the back of the fabric along the edge of the space you are filling in. Insert the needle across onto the opposite side of the shape. Bring your needle back up through the fabric right next to your starting hole on the original side of the shape. Repeat the process to fill the shape with stitches.

# Long and short stitch

The long and short stitch is great for filling large spaces. You can also change colors every couple of rows to get a blended effect.

**How to:** Work the first row of stitches along an edge of the shape you are filling. Alternate between long and short stitches, with the long stitches about ½" (1cm) in length and the short stitches about ¼" (6mm) in length. For the next row, work long stitches in the spaces created by the short stitches. Continue with the remaining rows.

# Laid stitch with cross-stitch couching

This is a superfun stitch that can fill in a large space quickly and looks pretty with an airy feel. You can use two colors of floss, which will make this stitch extra special.

**How to:** Stitch parallel lines about ½" (1cm) apart, back and forth at a 45-degree angle across the area you would like to fill. Repeat in the perpendicular direction. You should now have very long crisscrossing stitches.

Now you need a way to hold all of these stitches in place. You do this with cross-stitch couching stitches. If desired, you can switch floss colors.

**How to:** Bring your needle up from the back of the fabric closely above where two long threads cross. Insert your needle closely below where the two long threads cross, making a short vertical stitch. Bring your needle back up closely to the left of the two long threads and then insert it closely to the right of the two long threads, creating a short horizontal stitch. You should now have a little cross-stitch holding down the two long threads where they cross. Continue making cross-stitches at all the places where the long threads cross.

**Satin stitch**

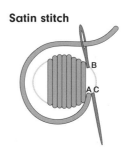

**Long and short stitch**

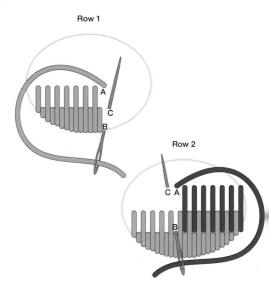

**Laid stitch with cross-stitch couching**

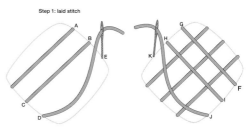

Step 1: laid stitch

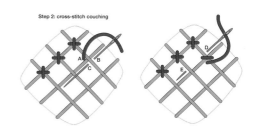

Step 2: cross-stitch couching

# Decorative Stitches

## *French knot*

I love the French knot for gussying up a project. And it's not as hard you might think!

**How to:** Bring your needle up from the back of the fabric. Hold the needle close to the starting point and angle the tip away from the starting point. Wrap the floss that is coming from the starting point around your needle twice. With your finger, hold the wrapped floss to the needle so it doesn't fall off. Insert the tip of your needle back into the fabric right next to the starting point (but not in the same hole). Pull your floss so that the wrapped floss on the needle is snug against the needle and laying against the fabric. Place your finger on the wrapped floss to hold the floss in place. Making sure to keep your finger on the wrapped floss, slowly pull your needle entirely through to the back and continue to pull gently until the knot is secure. Remove your finger from holding down the knot.

## *Single chain stitch*

Make a single chain stitch in the same way you would a row of chain stitches. After you make your first stitch, instead of continuing to make a row, make a tiny stitch over the loop, securing the loop in place (an anchoring stitch).

## *Lazy-daisy stitch*

A lazy-daisy stitch refers to several single chain stitches grouped together so they look like the petals of a flower.

**How to:** Start your lazy daisy by making a single chain stitch with the starting point at the center of the flower. Make additional single chain stitches beginning at the same starting point and working in a circle.

**French knot**

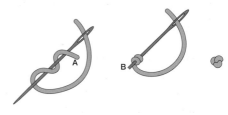

**Single chain stitch**

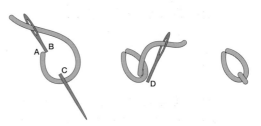

**Lazy-daisy stitch**

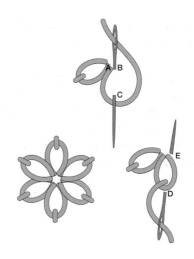

# Fly stitch

The fly stitch is a close cousin to the single chain stitch.

**How to:** Bring your needle up through from the back of the fabric. Instead of inserting your needle into the starting point like you would a single chain stitch, insert the needle a stitch length to the right of the starting point (about ¼" [6mm] in length), creating a wide loop. Bring your needle back up in between the two stitch points and a stitch length lower. Place the loop floss below the needle. Pull up on your needle, tightening the stitch, while also creating a "V" shape out of the loop. Make a tiny stitch over the loop, securing it in place (an anchoring stitch).

**Fly stitch**

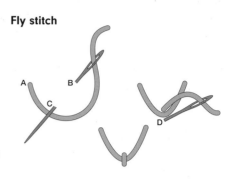

# Herringbone stitch

The herringbone stitch is similar to a cross-stitch but has slightly different proportions. The stitches run between two parallel lines, so it may be helpful to draw the lines on your fabric with a water-soluble marker.

Bring your needle up from the back of the fabric where you want to start on the first line. Insert the needle into the second line at a 45-degree angle from your first stitch. Bring your needle up from the back of the fabric on the second line and slightly backward (about ⅛" [3mm] in length) along the line. The next stitch will be the same as the first but in the opposite direction. Insert the needle back into the first line at a 45-degree angle; then bring the needle up from the back of the fabric on the first line and slightly backward along the line (about ⅛" [3mm] in length). Continue in the same manner to make a row of herringbone stitches.

**Herringbone stitch**

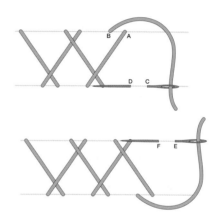

# Stitches for Edging
## Blanket stitch

The blanket stitch can provide a simple decorative edge to your fabric and can also be used as a surface embroidery.

**How to:** To start a row of blanket stitches on the edge of a fabric, bring your needle up from the back of the fabric ¼" (6mm) from the edge. Bring your needle around the edge and back through from the back at the same spot where you started, creating a loop around the edge. Bring your needle through the loop you just made sideways, from the right to the left, at the edge of the fabric. Now your thread is anchored, and you're ready to start your first blanket stitch. Insert your needle on the front of the fabric ¼" (6mm) from the edge and ¼" (6mm) to the right of your starter stitch. Bring your needle around the edge, from the back to the front and through the loop. Pull the stitch tight. Continue in the same manner to make blanket stitches around the edge of your fabric.

**Blanket stitch**

Starting a blanket stitch

Working a blanket stitch

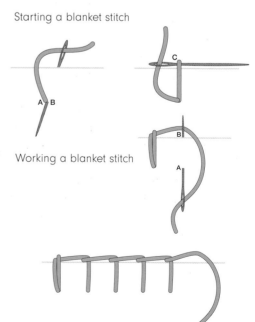

# Buttonhole stitch

A buttonhole stitch is similar and often confused with the blanket stitch. The main difference is that a buttonhole stitch makes a small knot, or purl, at the edge of the fabric, which helps protect it against the wear and tear of buttons. The stitches are also made closer together than a blanket stitch.

**How to:** To start a row of buttonhole stitches on an edge, bring your needle up from the back of the fabric ¼" (6mm) from the edge. Bring your needle around the edge and through from the back at the same spot where you started, creating a loop around the edge. Bring your needle through the loop you just made sideways, from the right to the left, at the edge of the fabric. Now your thread is anchored and you're ready to start your first buttonhole stitch. Bring your needle to the edge to the back of the fabric and come up to the front ¼" (6mm) from the edge and to the right, close to your starter stitch. Maneuver your needle so it comes up through the loop. Pull the loop tight, and as you pull, maneuver the knot (or purl) made in the process to the edge of the fabric. This is your first buttonhole stitch. Continue in the same manner around your buttonhole.

# Cross-Stitches
## Counted cross-stitch

Counted cross-stitch is usually done on a fabric that is woven evenly where the threads create small squares that form an easily countable grid. This grid mimics a counted cross-stitch pattern chart.

Find the center of your counted cross-stitch pattern chart and mark where you would like the center of your motif to be on the fabric with a water-soluble marker. Pick what color you'd like to start with and decide what row of stitches you'd like to start with. The square farthest to the left of a row of stitches will be your first stitch. Find that same square on your fabric using the center point as a guide. Bring your needle up through the bottom left-hand corner of the first square in the row. Insert it back through the fabric in the upper right-hand corner of the first square. Continue in the same manner across the row for the number of stitches in that row. To complete the stitches, bring the needle up in the bottom right-hand corner of the last square and then insert it into the top left corner. Continue back across the row. Continue in the same manner for the remainder of your pattern.

**Buttonhole stitch**

Starting a buttonhole stitch

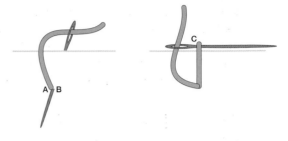

Working a buttonhole stitch

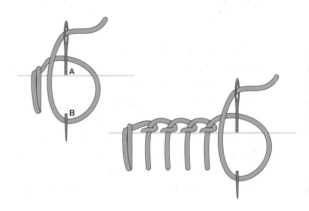

**Counted cross-stitch**

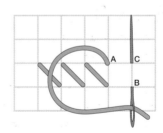

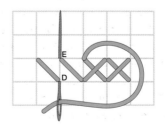

# Simple Sewing Techniques

## Cutting Techniques

### When to Use a Rotary Cutter

When a pattern calls for straight lines, strips, or a perfect rectangle or square, your best bet is to use a rotary cutter with a self-healing cutting mat and quilting ruler. It's much quicker and more precise than cutting with scissors.

### Squaring Up Your Fabric

The first rotary cut you'll want to make on a new piece of fabric is to square up your fabric—that is, to make sure you have a clean cut along the grain.

**How to:** To cut off a raw edge along the grain line, place the bulk of fabric on your left and the uneven edge on the right. Line up the fold of your fabric along a horizontal grid line on the cutting mat. Use the grid on the quilting ruler and mat to place the ruler exactly perpendicular to the folded edge of the fabric near the raw edge. Place the blade against the right edge of the ruler and move the cutter upward along the ruler with a little bit of pressure. Hold the ruler firmly in place as you cut, moving your hand up the ruler as needed to keep it in place. (If you're left-handed, just flip the directions. Have the bulk of the fabric on your right and cut on the left.)

### Cutting Strips and Rectangles

Now that you have a nice square edge, you can cut strips, rectangles and squares.

**How to cut strips:** Move your fabric so that your squared-up edge is laying along the vertical 0" (0cm) measurement on the cutting mat and your fold is still on a horizontal line. Use the guides to line up the ruler to the width of strip you'd like to cut. Cut the strip with your rotary cutter. Keep moving along the fabric to cut additional strips.

**How to cut rectangles (or squares):** First, cut a strip to the width you'd like your rectangles/squares to be. Next, rotate your strip so that the cut edge is laying along a horizontal line on the self-healing cutting mat. With your cutter and ruler, trim off the selvage edge from the strip. (The selvage doesn't stretch the same as the rest of the fabric, so you'll need to trim it off). Move the edge so it's on the vertical 0" (0cm) mark. Use the measurement guides on the mat to line up the ruler to the length of the rectangle/square you need, and cut. If you need more, continue cutting along the strip. Note: Because the strip is folded, you'll get two rectangles. If you need only one rectangle or square, open up the strip before cutting so you're cutting through only one layer of fabric.

### Clipping Curves and Corners

After you've sewn a curved seam or a corner, it's important to either reduce the bulk or add flexibility in the seam allowance so your piece lays flat when turned right-side out. Reduce bulk by clipping corners and cutting notches in outward curves (mountains). Clip inward curves (valleys) to add flexibility to the seam allowance.

**How to clip corners:** At the corner, cut off the seam allowance at a diagonal close to the seam (about 1⁄16" [2mm]).

**How to clip inward curves (valleys):** Make a snip into the seam allowance, almost reaching the seam (keep about 1⁄16" [2mm] away from the seam). Repeat every 1⁄2" (1cm) or so around the curve.

**How to cut notches in outward curves (mountains):** Cut a notch or small triangle out of the seam allowance 1⁄16" (2mm) from the seam and about every 1⁄2" (1cm) around the curve.

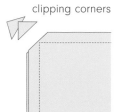
clipping corners

clipping curves

clipping notches

## Pinning

Fabric likes to move and stretch as it's sewn, and pinning will make sure that everything stays in place. This is especially important when you want two seams to line up.

**How to:** Line up your fabric edges and place a pin at the beginning and end of the seam you'd like to sew. Next, place pins around any seams you want to line up. Add pins every 2" (5cm) or so across the rest of the seam. For tricky corners or curves, add more pins.

## Knowing the Seam Allowance

The seam allowance is the the space between the stitch line and the raw edge of fabric. Unless otherwise stated, all seam allowances in this book are ¼" (6mm). To keep a consistent ¼" (6mm) seam allowance, use a ¼" (6mm) presser foot on your sewing machine, or measure ¼" (6mm) away from the needle and mark your machine's metal throat plate with a marker or piece of tape.

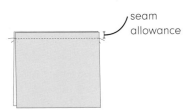

seam allowance

## Backstitching

Every seam made with a sewing machine in this book should start and end by backstitching (back tacking) the seam. Backstitching locks the threads at the end of a seam in place so they don't unravel when you work with your fabric.

**How to:** Start sewing your seam with a straight stitch, stopping after you've made 2 to 3 stitches. Press the reverse button or lever on your sewing machine and stitch back over the beginning stitches. Turn off the reverse and stitch to the end of your seam. When you reach the end of the seam, press the reverse and stitch back over the seam 2 to 3 stitches. Turn off the reverse and stitch over the last stitches again.

## Topstitching

Topstitching is a visible row of straight stitches usually seen next to a seam or at an opening to give a project a finished appearance. You'll see topstitching a lot in this book when you work on bags. Not only is it decorative, it holds the bag lining in place to give the opening a clean edge.

**How to:** Unless otherwise stated, to create a topstitch, use your sewing machine to stitch a row of straight stitches ⅛" (3mm) from the seam you want to topstitch next to. Because topstitching is visible, match the thread you use to the color of the outer fabric.

## Ladder Stitch

A ladder stitch is a hand stitch used to make a seam or close an opening, and, when tightened, the stitches appear to be almost invisible.

**How to:** Turn the raw edge of the seam allowance toward the inside of the opening. Tie a knot at the end of your thread and bring your needle up through the fabric on one side, ⅛" (3mm) from the start of the opening. Insert the needle directly across the opening from the side you're on. Guide your needle under the seam allowance fold ¼" (6mm) and come back up through the fabric to the front along the fold. Continue in the same manner, going back and forth across the opening. Leave your stitches loose as you go. When you've reached the other end of the opening, gently pull on your thread, pulling all of the stitches tight and closing the opening. Tie off your thread. To hide the end of the thread, insert your needle where you tied your knot and pull it up through the fabric at least 2" (5cm) away, then cut the end of the thread.

## Basting

Basting is a method of temporarily holding several layers of fabric together. This can be done with long hand stitches through the layers of fabric, with bent-arm safety pins, or by setting the sewing machine to the longest stitch.

# 2 *For the Home*

Add some warmth, happiness and even a little silliness to your home. Each project in this section was designed to help brighten your day, from the time you get up until the time you go to sleep. You'll find something for every room in your house. I love decorating with handmade items. It's such a wonderful feeling to know that your time, handiwork and love went into making a piece, and it's definitely what makes a house a home. Take a nap with a giant Skunk Floor Pillow, then host a dinner party with a no-sew Fox & Flowers Table Runner. Let your child splish and splash with the whale in the Whale Shower Curtain, then tuck them into an Octopus Quilt-covered bed. As you stitch the projects in this chapter, you'll learn how to hand-stitch a buttonhole, work with burlap and basic quilting techniqes.

# Wall Art
## "WHAT A LOVELY EVENING" OWL

SEWING SKILL LEVEL: **1**   EMBROIDERY SKILL LEVEL: **2**

● "What a lovely evening," said the owl as he nested in the ferns one summer night. This big owl embroidery makes a great compliment to the Barn Owl Throw Pillow (on page 44). It would definitely be the statement piece in any room. It is stitched with yarn and then upholstered to a prestretched canvas from your local art or craft store. Don't be afraid to use this concept with other motifs from this book. Yes, embroidery can be art!

## Supplies

### EMBROIDERY
- Basic Embroidery Kit for big stitches (see page 8)
- embroidery needle
- sewing thread
- yarn, worsted weight (suggested colors: lavender, light blue, pink, light brown, gray, olive, green)
- "What a Lovely Evening" Owl pattern (see page 33)

### FABRIC
- linen, white or light colored: 30" x 35" (76cm x 89cm)
- batting, low loft: 30" x 35" (76cm x 89cm) (cut from 1 yard or from a package of standard "crib size" batting)

### SEWING, ETC.
- scissors
- rotary cutter
- quilting ruler
- self-healing cutting mat
- water-soluble marker
- prestretched canvas: 20" x 24" x 1½" (51cm x 61cm x 4cm)
- staple gun and staples
- hot-glue gun and glue
- picture hanging D-rings and screws
- picture wire

**See page 116 for the "What a Lovely Evening" Owl stitch and color guide**

## EMBROIDER THE MOTIF

1 Transfer the Owl pattern to your linen. (See the techniques on page 16 as needed.) Then place the linen on top of the batting. Using the embroidery needle and thread, baste together the two layers with long, random stitches across the fabric.

2 Place the linen/batting in the embroidery hoop and, using the yarn and needle, embroider your Owl motif. Refer to the stitch and color guide on page 116, the stitch library on pages 20–25 and the techniques on pages 18–19 as needed. When you are finished, cut and pull out the basting stitches.

next step ▶

## MOUNT TO THE PRE-STRETCHED CANVAS

**3** Center your embroidery on top of the front of the pre-stretched canvas. With a water-soluble marker, place a few marks to signify the corners and sides of the canvas.

**4** Holding by the sides, flip the embroidery and canvas over onto a flat surface (embroidery facing down). Check that your marks are still lined up with the canvas. Wrap the top center of the fabric over to the back of the canvas and place one staple through the fabric and into the canvas frame, holding the fabric in place.

**5** Wrap the bottom center of the fabric over to the back of the canvas and place one staple into the canvas frame. Repeat with the two centers of the sides. Continue pulling and stapling around the entire perimeter of the canvas, but avoid stapling the sides closer than 3" (8cm) from the corners. Make sure to turn over and check the front often to make sure the embroidery fabric is stretching evenly without creating puckers.

**6** Cut away the batting layer at the corners by cutting out a square of batting at each corner.

**7** Wrap the corner of the linen over the corner of the canvas and staple in place. Wrap either side of each corner to the the back, flattening the bulk as you wrap to make a nice, clean corner. Staple in place.

**8** Trim the linen/batting on the back of the canvas so that it hangs over the frame by just 1" (2cm). Tack the edge in place to the edge of the canvas frame with the glue gun.

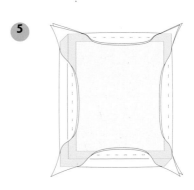

## ATTACH THE PICTURE WIRE

**9** On the back of the canvas, mark one side about 6"–8" (15cm–20cm) from the top. Measure the distance and mark the second side in the same place. Screw a D-ring into the canvas frame at a 45-degree angle, pointing upward. Repeat on the other side with the second D-ring.

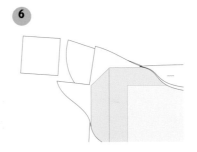

**10** Take the end of the picture wire and thread it through one of the D-rings. Twist the end around the length of wire several times. Repeat on the other side, trimming and twisting the wire, leaving a bit of slack in the wire for hanging.

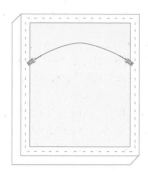

**"What a Lovely Evening" Owl Pattern**

Enlarge pattern 300%
Actual size: 18.25" x 20.25"
(46cm x 51cm)

# Table Runner
## FOX & FLOWERS

SEWING SKILL LEVEL: **1**    EMBROIDERY SKILL LEVEL: **3**

- Let this embroidered fox run wild across your dining room table. Nestled in a field of wildflowers and grasses, this quirky fox makes a super cute accent piece for any casual dinner party. The table runner is made with yarn that's embroidered with large stitches onto burlap and sports decorative fringed edges. Believe it or not, there is no machine sewing in this project—it's all about the embroidery!

## Supplies

### EMBROIDERY

- pencil or pen
- tear-away fusible embroidery stabilizer
- tapestry needle
- yarn, worsted weight (suggested colors: green, lime green, yellow-orange, white, black, orange, red, purple)

- Fox & Flowers pattern (see page 122)
- iron

### FABRIC

- burlap in white (or brown if you prefer): ½ yard (46cm) (assuming a 45"-52" [114cm x 132cm] bolt) or 45" x 18" (114cm x 46cm)

### SEWING, ETC.

- sewing scissors

**See page 116 for the Fox & Flowers stitch and color guide**

### PREP THE BURLAP

1 Start by straightening the long edges of the burlap and getting rid of messy edges. To do so, locate a long strand of burlap that goes across the entire edge of one long side near the edge. Snip the short edge on either side of the long strand. Pull the one long burlap strand all the way out of the fabric. This will create a straight line space across the burlap. Cut down the center of that space, giving you a straight edge. Repeat for the other long edge of the burlap. Press the burlap using medium heat.

### EMBROIDER THE MOTIF

2 Enlarge the Fox pattern and transfer it onto the tear-away fusible embroidery stabilizer. (See the enlarging and transferring techniques on page 16 as needed.) Lay the stabilizer, adhesive side down, on the burlap, making sure that the Fox motif is in the center of the fabric. Following the instructions on the package, fuse the stabilizer to the burlap.

3 Using the needle and yarn, embroider the Fox & Flowers motif through the burlap and stabilizer. Refer to the stitch and color guide on page 116 and the stitch library on pages 20–25 as needed. After you're finished with the embroidery, carefully tear away the stabilizer. (Refer to the techniques on page 16 as needed.)

### FINISH THE EDGES

4 For a fringed look, pull out the strands on the long edges of the burlap, row by row, until your desired fringe length is reached. Repeat the same process on the short (selvage) edges of the burlap. You may need to follow the instructions in step 1 to create a raw edge to unravel.

1a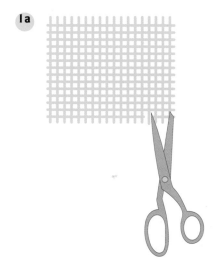

1b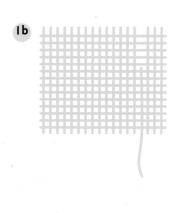

1c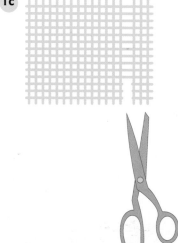

# Coffee Cozy
## WOODLAND CREATURES

● Don't grab a disposable paper sleeve on your next coffee run; use this sweet reusable one instead! Environmentally friendly and adorable—what more could you want with your morning joe? This coffee cozy is home to a tiny and sweet birdie, bunny and hedgehog. In case you miss the look of a typical coffee sleeve, just turn your cozy inside out to reveal the corduroy, which mimics the familiar corrugated paper. Embellish your coffee cozy with a big button, and you'll be ready to keep your latte warm and your hands cool.

## Supplies

### EMBROIDERY
- Basic Embroidery Kit (see page 8)
- six-strand embroidery floss (suggested colors: bright blue, pink, black, red, yellow-orange, brown, purple, light blue, medium green, lime green)

### FABRIC
- white or cream quilt-weight cotton or linen for the front (embroidery): at least 16" x 12" (41cm x 30cm) (cut from ⅓ yard [31cm] or one fat quarter)
- tan corduroy (or patterned quilt-weight fabric) for the back: at least 14" x 5" (36cm x 13cm). Corduroy lines should be parallel to the 5" (13cm) edge. (Cut from ¼ yard [23cm] or one fat quarter)

### SEWING, ETC.
- Basic Sewing Kit (see page 11)
- seam ripper
- button: 1½" (4cm)

**See page 116 for Woodland Creatures stitch and color guide**

## EMBROIDER THE MOTIF

1   Transfer the Woodland Creatures pattern onto your front fabric. (See the techniques on page 16 as needed.) Make sure to include the coffee cozy template and all markings.

2   Place the front in the embroidery hoop and, using the floss and needle, embroider your Woodland Creatures motif. Refer to the stitch and color guide on page 116, the stitch library on pages 20–25 and the techniques on pages 18–19 as needed.

next step →

## ASSEMBLE THE COZY

**3** Place front and back fabrics wrong sides together. Then cut along the cozy template markings on the front fabric.

**4** With right sides together, pin and machine sew around the entire edge, leaving the marked gap open. Clip the corners. Cut notches in the outward curve and clip the inward curve. Turn the coffee cozy right-side out through the opening.

**5** Tuck in the raw edges of the opening ¼" (6mm) toward the inside and pin in place. Topstitch around the entire edge of the coffee cozy ⅛" (3mm) from the edge, sewing shut the opening in the process.

## STITCH THE BUTTONHOLE

**6** To determine the size of the buttonhole, measure the diameter of the button and then add the depth. With a water-soluble pen, draw a horizontal line the length of that measurement on the front of the coffee cozy about ¾" (2cm) from the right edge, centered vertically.

**7** With the sewing machine, sew ⅛" (3mm) around each side of the line, making a rectangle. Then carefully slice open the center of the buttonhole using a seam ripper.

**8** Use the floss color of your choice to stitch the buttonhole. Make one backstitch with the embroidery floss within the rectangle around your slash on the back fabric. This will hold the floss in place while you stitch. Starting on the left edge, bring the needle up through the slash between the front and back fabrics. Using a buttonhole stitch, stitch along the side of the slash.

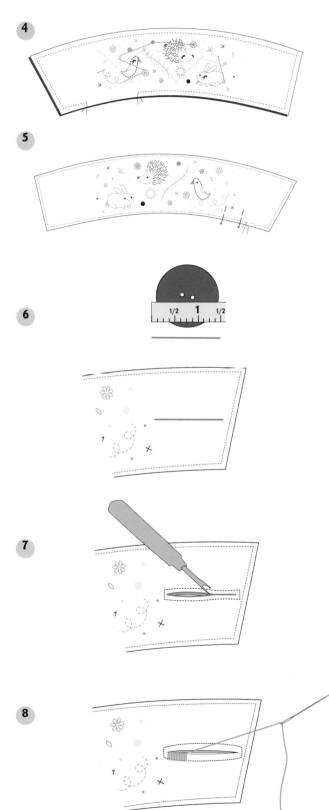

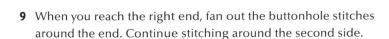

**9** When you reach the right end, fan out the buttonhole stitches around the end. Continue stitching around the second side.

**10** When you get to end of the second side and back to where you started, finish the buttonhole with a bar tack. To make a bar tack, make a stitch across the entire height of the two sides at the left end of the slash. Blanket stitch around the long stitch and the layers of fabric. Tie off the end of the floss, and the buttonhole is complete.

**11** Lay your button on the left front of the coffee cozy, centered vertically, ⅛" (3mm) from the left edge. Using a water-soluble pen, mark the center of the button on the coffee cozy. Using the embroidery floss color of your choice, stitch the button to the coffee cozy. Your coffee cozy is now complete!

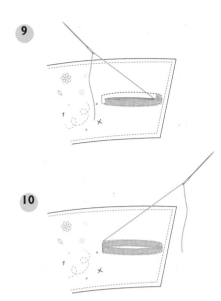

# Floor Pillow
## SKUNK

• Who says you can't cuddle up with a skunk? This sweet floor pillow is a fun and simple large embroidery project. The pillow's patterned gusset gives the pillow depth, making it big and cuddly. Embroider the smiling skunk with his butterfly friend to the front of the linen pillow with yarn, and on the back, use your favorite colored linen or patterned fabric.

# Supplies

## EMBROIDERY
• Basic Embroidery Kit for big stitches (see page 8)
• Skunk pattern (see page 43)
• yarn, worsted weight (suggested colors: blue, white, black, orange, purple, green)

## FABRIC
• linen, light or medium color (for the front/embroidery): 1 yard (92cm)
• pattern/solid quilt-weight cotton, cotton flannel or linen for pillow back: 1 yard (92cm)
• pattern/solid quilt-weight cotton for gusset: ½ yard (46cm)

## SEWING, ETC.
• Basic Sewing Kit (see page 11)
• water-soluble marker
• stuffing: about 3 pounds (½ kg)

**See page 116 for Skunk stitch and color guide**

## EMBROIDER THE MOTIF

1 Enlarge the Skunk pattern and transfer it onto the light-colored linen fabric (the pillow front). (See the techniques on page 16 as needed.) Place the linen in the large quilting hoop and, using the yarn and needle, embroider your skunk motif. Refer to the stitch and color guide on page 116, the stitch library on pages 20–25 and the techniques on pages 18–19 as needed.

## CUT THE FRONT AND BACK

2 With a water-soluble marker, draw a line around your embroidery about 4" (10cm) from the edge of the motif. Add notches to your line at approximately 12" (30cm) intervals.

3 Layer your embroidered linen and patterned fabrics (for the back) with wrong sides together. Cut through both pieces along the drawn line, being careful to also cut out the notches.

**2**   **3**

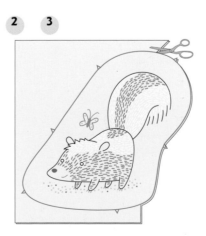

next step

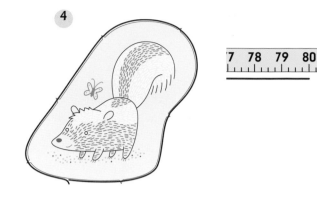

## CREATE THE GUSSET STRIP

To measure the length around your shape, lay a piece of thread along the edge of the shape. Then measure how long the thread is. Make a note of your measurement.

Cut three ½" (1cm) strips from your gusset fabric along the long edge. Join the strips using a diagonal seam. It may be helpful to draw the diagonal line on the wrong side of one of your fabrics as a guide and sew directly on that line. Cut off the excess fabric, leaving a ¼" (6mm) seam allowance. Iron the seam open. Continue to add strips until your gusset measures the length you recorded in step 4, plus an additional 5" (13cm).

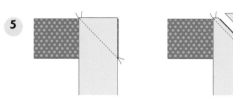

## SEW THE PILLOW

With right sides together, and starting at the bottom, carefully pin the gusset along the edge of the pillow front. The ends of the gusset will overlap. Starting 5" (13cm) away from where the ends of the gusset overlap, sew the gusset onto the front with a ¼" (6mm) seam allowance. Stop sewing when you're 5" (13cm) away from where the gusset overlaps on the other side.

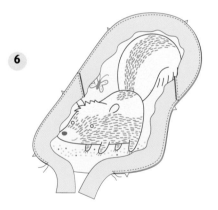

Trim the ends of the gusset so that the ends overlap by 3½" (9cm). With right sides together, angle the ends of the gusset perpendicular to each other. Pin them together and join using a diagonal seam. Cut off the excess fabric, leaving a ¼" (6mm) seam allowance. Sew the remaining edge of the gusset to the pillow front.

On the unsewn edge of the gusset, make a mark with

the water-soluble pen directly across from each notch on the pillow front.

With right sides together, carefully pin the gusset to the back fabric. Line up the marks on the gusset with the notches on the pillow back. Sew along the edge, leaving a 5" (13cm) opening at the bottom. Try not to make the opening land on one of the gusset strip seams.

Clip into the seam allowance on the inward curves and cut notches on the outward curves.

## FINISH AND STUFF

Turn the pillow right-side out through the opening. With your stuffing, stuff the skunk pillow through the opening. Stuff little by little to get the stuffing even throughout.

Hand-sew shut the opening using a ladder stitch (see page 27 as needed).

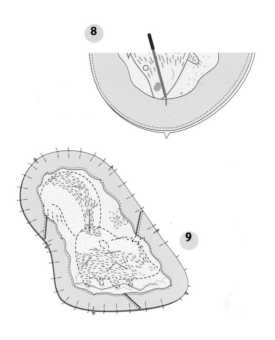

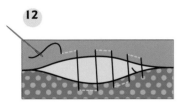

**Skunk Pattern**
Enlarge 400%
Actual size: 21" x 20" (53cm x 51cm)

# Throw Pillow
## BARN OWL

- The crewel embroidery style of owl pillows popular in the 70s inspired this throw pillow. It would make a great addition to your sofa. Pair it with the "What a Lovely Evening" Owl Wall Art project (on page 30) for an owl-tastic room. This vintage modern pillow features a sweet barn owl embroidered onto gray linen and has a simple, envelope style back.

## Supplies

### EMBROIDERY
- Basic Embroidery Kit for big stitches (see page 8)
- yarn, worsted weight (suggested colors: white, tan, orange, light teal, black
- Barn Owl pattern (see page 122)

### FABRIC
- linen, light or medium color, for front (embroidery): 20" x 20" (51cm x 51cm) (cut from ¾ yard [69cm])
- muslin for lining: 12½" x 12½" (32cm x 32cm) (cut from ½ yard [46cm] or fat quarter)
- quilt-weight cotton for back: 12½" x 18" (32cm x 46cm) (cut from ½ yard [46cm] or fat quarter)

### SEWING, ETC.
- Basic Sewing Kit (see page 11)
- rotary cutter
- quilting ruler
- self-healing cutting mat
- water-soluble marker
- damp cloth
- pillow form: 12½" x 12½" (32cm x 32cm)

**See page 116 for Barn Owl stitch and color guide**

## EMBROIDER THE MOTIF

1   Enlarge and transfer the Barn Owl pattern to your linen fabric. (See the techniques on page 16 as needed.) Center the motif on the fabric.

2   Place the linen in the embroidery hoop and, using the yarn and needle, embroider your Barn Owl motif. Refer to the stitch and color guide on page 116, the stitch library on pages 20–25 and the techniques on pages 18–19 as needed.

next step

## CUT THE FABRIC

**3** Using your quilting ruler, self-healing cutting mat and a water-soluble marker, carefully draw a 12½" x 12½" (32cm x 32cm) square around your embroidery motif. Cut out the square using the rotary cutter. Remove any marker lines with a damp cloth. Set aside.

**4** Using your quilting ruler, self-healing cutting mat and rotary cutter, cut your back fabric into two 12½" x 9" (32cm x 23cm) pieces.

## ASSEMBLE THE COVER

**5** Hem one 12½" (32cm) edge of each back piece. To do so, fold the edge ½" (1cm) and press it. Next, fold the edge ½" (1cm) again and press it. Then sew the hem in place using a ¼" (6mm) seam allowance.

**6** Lay the 12½" x 12½" (32cm x 32cm) muslin fabric piece on a flat surface and place the embroidered fabric piece on top of it with the embroidery facing up. This is your new pillow front (the embroidery is the "right" side, and the muslin is the "wrong" side).

**7** Place one back piece right-sides together with the new front piece. Match the 12½" (32cm) raw edge of the back piece to the top edge of the embroidered fabric.

**8** Place the other back piece right-sides together with the new front piece. Match the 12½" (32cm) raw edge of the back piece to the bottom edge of the embroidered fabric. The hemmed edges of the back pieces will overlap. Sew around the entire pillow using a ¼" (6mm) seam allowance.

**9** Turn the pillowcase right-side out through the opening between the back pieces. Insert the pillow form.

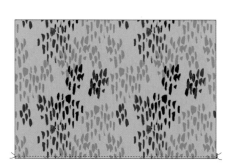

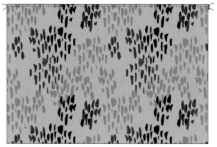

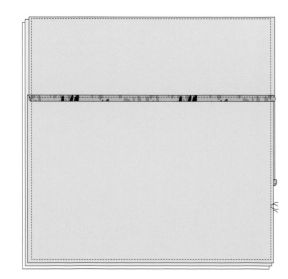

# Second Stitches
## GREAT HORNED OWL

● Meet the Barn Owl's cousin, the Great Horned Owl. Stitch it onto white linen instead of gray for a fresh look.

**Great Horned Owl Pattern**
Enlarge 250%
Actual size:
12" x 12" (30cm x 30cm)

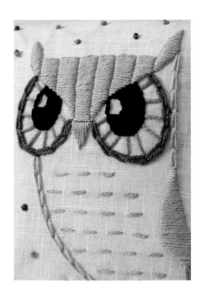

**Great Horned Owl Stitch and Color Guide**

dots: French knots
eyes: backstitch or one long stitch
wings, eyes, beaks: satin stitch
thick lines: chain stitch
dashed lines: running stitch

Satin stitch in columns
Stitch several columns
of satin stitches next
to each other for the
face and ears

# Shower Curtain
## WHALE

SEWING SKILL LEVEL: *3*   EMBROIDERY SKILL LEVEL: *3*

- Add some fun to a bland bathroom with this whale-themed shower curtain. The curtain is made with alternating bands of soft gray and white linen and has a huge smiling whale stitched on the front with yarn. By using French seams, your curtain will have beautiful edges with no raw threads hanging out. If your shower doesn't need a pick-me-up, relocate the curtain to the bedroom and have it stand in as a splashy closet door.

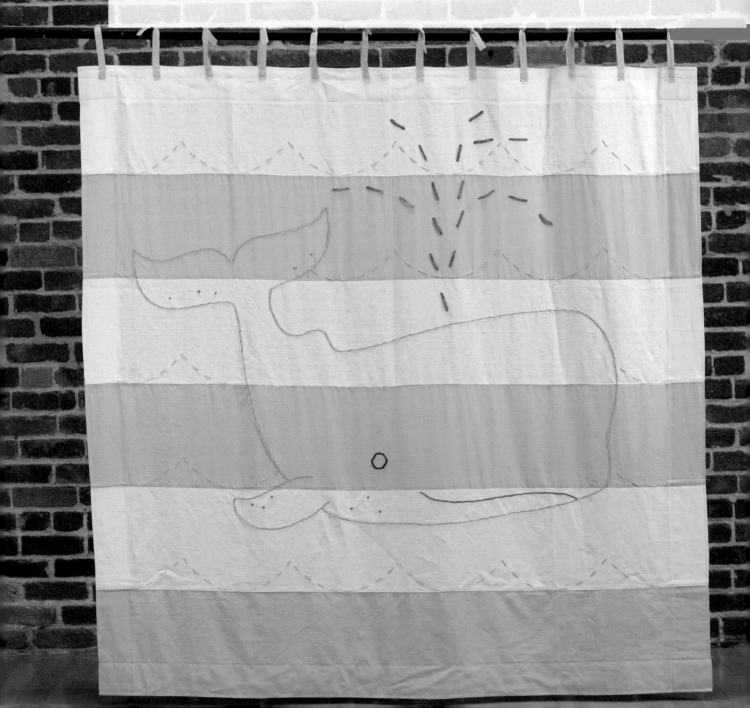

# Supplies

## EMBROIDERY

- Basic Embroidery Kit for big stitches (see page 8)
- yarn, worsted weight (suggested colors: light blue, olive, orange, cream, light tan, black)

## FABRIC

- linen, light color (or quilt-weight cotton if you prefer*): 3 yards (2.7m) (assuming at least a 48" [122cm] wide bolt**)
- linen, slightly darker color like gray or tan (or quilt-weight cotton if you prefer*): 3 yards (2.7m) (assuming at least a 48" [122cm] wide bolt**)

## SEWING, ETC.

- Basic Sewing Kit (see page 11)
- rotary cutter
- quilting ruler
- self-healing cutting mat

*Linen is better for this project because of its bolt size (see note below), but you can also use quilt-weight cotton.

**Measurement assumes at least a 48"

(122cm) wide bolt. You can, however, make this project with 3 yards (2.7m) of a 42" (107cm) wide bolt (for example, if you choose to use quilt-weight cotton). You'll need to add 5" (13cm) of patchwork to the top stripe of the shower curtain to make up for the shorter width.

**See page 117 for the Whale stitch and color guide**

## CUT THE FABRIC

1  Cut both 3-yard pieces of linen down to 88" (224cm) so you have two pieces, one light and one dark, measuring 88" x 48" (224cm x 122cm). Set aside the remaining 20" (51cm) from each linen piece.

2  Cut the light-colored 88" (224cm) pieces lengthwise into two pieces measuring 13" x 88" (33cm x 224cm) and one piece measuring 20½" x 88" (52cm x 224cm). Set aside the excess fabric. Repeat with the dark-colored 88" (224cm) linen piece.

## ASSEMBLE USING FRENCH SEAMS

Note: French seams refer to a process in which the raw edges of a seam are enclosed within another seam. Using French seams will allow your shower curtain to have beautiful seams on the back with no raw edges.

3  With wrong sides together, pin the 20½" (52cm) light-colored strip to one of the 13" (33cm) dark-colored strips, matching the 88" (224cm) edges. Sew along the edge using a ¼" (6mm) seam allowance.

4  Press the seam allowance in one direction. Then fold the fabric along the seam so that the right sides are facing each other. Press along the seam.

5  With right sides still together, sew along the folded

3

next step

seam using a ½" (1cm) seam allowance. Your first French seam is finished, and you should have a nice clean seam with no raw edges.

**6** Repeat steps 3–5 to make French seams with the remaining pieces. First, sew a light- and a dark-colored 13" (33cm) strip together; then sew the remaining light-colored 13" (33cm) and the dark-colored 20½" (52cm) strip together. When you are finished, you should have three sets of two strips.

Now sew the three sets together using French seams. The stripes should alternate between light- and dark-colored strips, with the 20½" (52cm) strips at the top and bottom. Once assembled, press all the seams in one direction.

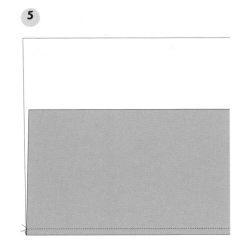

## HEM THE EDGES

**7** Square up the edges so that all the edges are straight and even.

**8** With wrong sides together, fold the edge of one of the side seams over 8" (20cm), measuring and pressing as you go. Unfold the edge. Fold the edge again 4" (10cm) so it meets the 8" (20cm) fold. Press. Refold along the 8" (20cm) fold line.

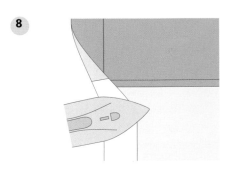

**9** Pin the hem and sew two seams: one on each side of the hem, ½" (1cm) from the edge. Repeat steps 8–9 for the other side, as well as the bottom (the dark-colored strip).

**10** Repeat steps 8–9 again for the top (light-colored edge), but only sew ½" (1cm) from the lower edge of the 4" (10cm) seam, leaving the pins in place. Set aside.

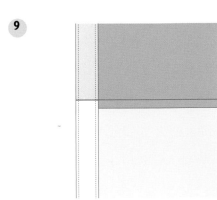

## MAKE THE HEADER TIES

**11** From the remaining dark-colored linen, cut 24 12" x 3" (30cm x 8cm) strips. Take one strip and, with wrong sides together, fold over one of the short edges ½" (1cm) and press. Repeat with the other short edge.

**12** Fold and press the entire strip in half lengthwise with wrong sides together. Unfold the strip. With wrong sides together, fold one of the long edges to the crease and press. Repeat with the other long edge.

**Illustration Color Key**

| Light linen fabric | | Dark linen fabric | |
|---|---|---|---|
| right side | | right side | |
| wrong side | | wrong side | |

Refold the handle along the original lengthwise crease. Sew around all of the edges using a ⅛" (3mm) seam allowance. Repeat with the remaining strips, creating 24 header ties.

13  On the top hem of the shower curtain, using a water-soluble marker, place 12 marks along the edge to indicate the header tie placement. (There will be two ties at each mark, so you need only 12 instead of 24.) The first and last mark should measure 3" (8cm) from the finished side edges, and the remaining 10 marks should be 6" (15cm) apart. Adjust the spaces as needed so that they are all the same width.

14  Draw a line along the top edge 1½" (4cm) from the top on both the front and back sides. Pin two header ties at each marking, aligning the bottom (short) end of each tie to the 1½" (4cm) line. Pin one header tie to the front of the curtain and one to the back side.

15  Sew across the top edge ½" (1cm) from the edge, sewing the header ties in place as you go. Sew another line 1¼" (3cm) from the top edge, sewing over the header ties again.

## EMBROIDER THE MOTIF

16  Using a water-soluble marker, enlarge and transfer the Whale motif onto the front of the curtain using the grid method of enlarging a pattern. The height of each curtain stripe represents the height of a grid square. To create a grid, draw a vertical line down the center of the curtain. Draw more vertical lines 12" (30cm) apart on each side of the center line to finish the grid on the curtain. Continue with the grid method of enlarging a pattern to transfer the Whale onto the curtain. (See the techniques on page 16 as needed.) Place the fabric in the quilting hoop and, using the yarn and needle, embroider your Whale motif. Refer to the stitch and color guide on page 117, the stitch library on pages 20–25 and the techniques on pages 18–19 as needed. (Note: Because the back of your embroidery will be visible, avoid jumping from one area to another using the same piece of yarn. To make the back look neat, finish off an area, and then start the new area with a fresh piece of yarn. Also use a waste knot or an away knot to start each piece of yarn (see pages 18–19 as needed).

12a
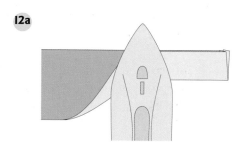

12b
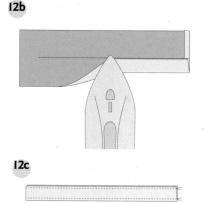

12c

14
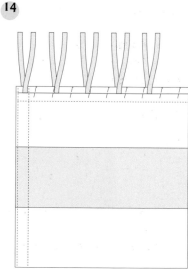

15
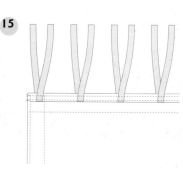

# Twin Quilt and Pillow Sham
## OCTOPUS

SEWING SKILL LEVEL: *3*

EMBROIDERY SKILL LEVEL: *3*

• Snuggle up with this Octopus Quilt and Pillow combo. Lie on top, and he will give you a hug; crawl underneath, and you'll become the head of the octopus. This twin-size quilt is great for a child's room, or use it as a lap quilt for yourself. The quilt is made using large embroidery stitched with yarn. The combination of the simple patchwork top and the hand-tied quilting technique makes this a simple design for the beginning quilter.

# Supplies

## EMBROIDERY

- Basic Embroidery Kit for big stitches (see page 8)
- yarn, worsted weight (suggested: coral orange, light teal, dark blue, tan)
- Fish and Suction Cup patterns (see page 57)
- water-soluble marker

## FABRIC

- white linen for quilt and pillow top: 1½ (1.4m) yards (42" [107cm] wide)
- off-white linen for quilt and pillow top: 3 yards (2.7m) (42" [107cm] wide)
- tan linen for quilt and pillow top: 1¾ yard (1.6m) (42" [107cm] wide)
- quilt-weight cotton fabric, three different patterns for quilt backing: 2 yards (2m) each
- muslin for pillow-top backing: muslin at least 33" x 27" (84cm x 69cm) (cut from 1 yard [92 cm])
- quilt-weight cotton fabric for pillow envelope: ¾ yard (69cm)
- quilt-weight cotton fabric for binding: 1 yard (92cm)
- batting: standard queen-size package, or 90" x 108" (229cm x 274cm) in your choice of loft and fiber

## SEWING, ETC.

- Basic Sewing Kit (see page 11)
- rotary cutter
- quilting ruler
- self-healing cutting mat
- painter's, quilter's or masking tape
- curved quilting safety pins
- size 8 Pearl cotton floss (three 95-yard [87m] balls) in white or off-white
- sharp hand-sewing needle

**See page 117 for Octopus grid assembly, stitch and color guide**

## SEWING YOUR QUILT AND PILLOW TOP

1   Using your rotary cutter, quilting ruler and self-healing cutting mat, cut your linen fabrics into 10½" (27cm) strips. Cut the strips crosswise to make 10½" (27cm) squares. For the quilt and pillow top, you need a total of 19 white squares, 35 off-white squares and 15 tan squares.

2   Lay out your squares in nine rows, using the assembly diagram on the Octopus stitch guide (see page 117) as reference. Label each row 1–9. With right sides together, machine stitch the squares in each row with a ¼" (6mm) seam allowance. Make sure to keep your squares in order.

3   Iron the seam allowances in the odd-numbered rows to the left and the even-numbered rows to the right.

4   Pin together row 1 to row 2. With right sides together, line up the seams at the points of the squares. Because the seam allowances were pressed in opposite directions, the seams should nest together. Place a pin directly through the seam, ensuring that the points of the squares line up exactly. Add additional pins between the points, holding the rest of the row together. Sew together the two rows with a ¼" (6mm) seam allowance. Repeat with all of the remaining rows. Press the seam allowances in the same direction and then turn the quilt top over and iron the front.

**2**

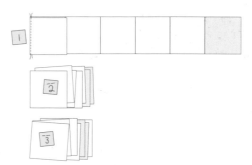

**4**

next step

**5**  Repeat the process in steps 2–4 for the pillow top.

**6**  Fold the pillow top in half along the short edge. Trim 2" (5cm) off of the (unfolded) edge, cutting through both layers. Unfold the pillow top.

**6**

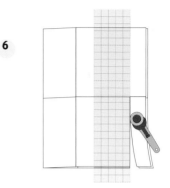

## EMBROIDER THE MOTIF

**7**  Using a water-soluble marker, enlarge and transfer the Octopus motif onto the quilt and pillow top using the grid method of enlarging a pattern. Each square in the quilt and pillow top represents a square on the grid. Refer to the stitch and color guide on page 117, the stitch library on pages 20–25 and the techniques on pages 18–19 as needed. Also transfer the Fish and Suction Cup motifs to your quilt using the patterns.

**8**  Place the quilt top in the quilting hoop and, using yarn and the needle, embroider the Octopus motif. Refer to the stitch and color guide on page 117 and the techniques on pages 18–19 as needed.

## ASSEMBLE THE BACKING

**9**  Assign your three quilt backing fabrics letters A, B and C. Refer to the quilt backing diagram (at right) for the fabric layout. Cut your three quilt backing fabric pieces to 38" (97cm) wide. Cut the fabric in row 2 to 30½" (77cm) long. Cut the fabric in rows 1 and 3 to 33" (84cm) long. Set aside the scraps to use in the next section. Sew together your quilt backing fabrics into rows and then sew the rows together in the same way you made your quilt front in steps 2–4.

**Quilt Backing Diagram**

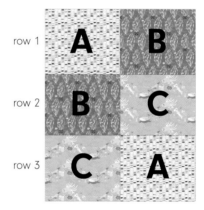

row 1

row 2

row 3

## MAKE THE QUILT (AND PILLOW) "SANDWICH"

**10**  Lay your quilt back, right-side down, on a large flat surface. Smooth out the fabric and tape the edges to the surface to keep it in position. Try not to stretch the fabric as you tape it. Lay the batting on top of the quilt back, lining up a corner of the batting with a corner of the quilt backing with about ½" (1cm) of the quilt backing edge still visible. Trim the batting on the other two sides so it lays flat on the quilt backing, with ½" (1cm) of the quilt backing visible all the way around. Take the quilt top and center it on the quilt backing and batting with the right side up. Using curved quilting safety pins, and starting from the center of your quilt top, pin through all the layers of your "sandwich." Work outward, pinning and smoothing the quilt top as you go. Work carefully and use a pin at least every 8" (20cm). When you're finished, remove the tape from your backing. Set aside.

**10**

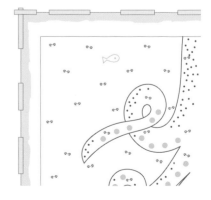

**11**  To add a border to your pillow top, start by cutting, from your backing fabric scraps, four 1" (2.5cm) strips, two of them 21" (53cm) long and the other two 29" (74cm) long. With right sides together, line up the long edge of a 21" (53cm) strip with a short side of the pillow top, centering the strip on the pillow top. Pin and sew the strip to the pillow top. Press the seam allowance toward the strip, then trim off the ends so they are even with the pillow top.

12 Using the illustration (right) as a guide, continue in the same manner to sew the second 21" (53cm) strip to the other short side of the pillow top, and the 29" (74cm) strips to the long sides.

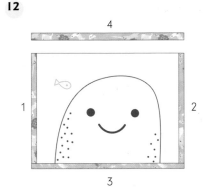

13 To create a single batting piece for your pillow, gather strips of batting scraps leftover from your quilt. Using sewing thread and the needle, loosely stitch them together (side by side, not overlapping) with very large stitches. Trim the assembled batting to 32" x 26" (81cm 66cm). Sandwich your 33" x 27" (84cm x 69cm) muslin pillow-top "backing" fabric, batting and pillow top in the same way as you did in step 10.

## MAKE THE QUILTING STITCHES

14 Thread your Pearl cotton floss through your hand-stitching needle and double up the floss by bringing the end toward the spool. Trim your floss so that your doubled floss is about 3 feet long with the ends meeting. Bring your needle through your quilt sandwich from the top to the bottom, leaving the ends about 4" (10cm) long on the top of the quilt. Bring the needle back through your sandwich from the bottom to the top about ⅛" (3mm) from where you started.

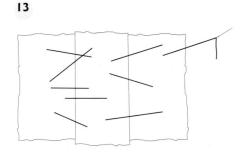

15 Repeat step 14, making your next stitch about 6" (15cm) from the last stitch. Continue until you run out of floss on your needle, making sure to end on the top of the quilt with at least 3" (8cm) of floss left on the needle.

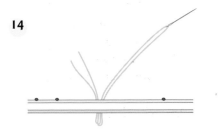

16 Cut the floss right below the needle to release the needle from the floss loop. On the top of the quilt, cut the floss in the center of each of the long stitches. Then tie the ends of each stitch into a knot twice. Repeat with the other floss ends. Trim the ends of the ties so that they are about 1" (2cm) long. Continue steps 15–16 over the entire quilt and pillow top.

## BIND THE QUILT

17 Cut your binding fabric into 2½" (6cm) strips. (You can use one binding fabric for all of your binding or use several different fabrics for the binding, like I did, for a patchwork look.) Join the strips using a diagonal seam. It may be helpful to draw the diagonal line on the wrong side of one of your fabrics as a guide and sew directly on that line. Cut off the excess fabric, leaving a ¼" (6mm) seam allowance. Iron the seam open. Continue adding the remaining strips until the binding measures the distance around the entire quilt top, plus at least 18" (46cm) more.

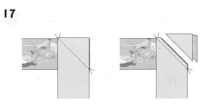

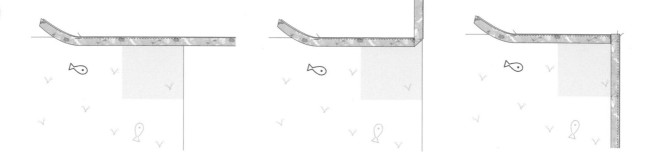

**18** Fold and iron the entire length of the binding in half lengthwise with the wrong sides together.

**19** Using your rotary cutter, quilting ruler and self-healing cutting mat, trim the excess batting and backing fabric from your quilt so that the edges lines up with the edges of the quilt front. Make sure to keep your corners square.

**20** Starting on one side of your quilt, and leaving a 6" (15cm) tail of your binding free, match the raw edges of the binding with the raw edge of the quilt top. Sew the binding to your quilt with ½" (1cm) seam allowance. Make sure you sew through all your layers. Stop sewing ½" (1cm) before reaching the first corner. Backstitch and remove the quilt from the machine.

Rotate your quilt counterclockwise 90 degrees so that the attached binding is on top. Fold the tail straight up so that the edge is parallel to the next side that will be bound, making a 45-degree fold in your binding.

Next, fold the loose binding down, creating a fold that is flush with the top of the quilt. Continue sewing on this new side ½" (1cm) in from the corner on either side of the quilt, starting at the place where your last seam ended.

**21** Continue sewing the binding around your quilt, making your corners the same as you did in step 20. Stop sewing 6" (15cm) from the end of the starting tail. Overlap the starting tail and remaining binding, laying them flat against the quilt edge. Trim the excess binding so that the ends overlap by 2½" (6cm).

Unfold the two binding tails. With right sides together, place the ends together at a 90-degree angle. Pin and join the strips using a diagonal seam. It may be helpful to draw the diagonal line on the wrong side of one of your fabrics as a guide and sew directly on that line. Cut off the excess fabric, leaving a ¼" (6mm) seam allowance. Refold your binding and sew the remaining edge to the quilt.

2½"

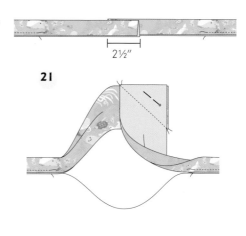

**21**

**22a**

**22b**

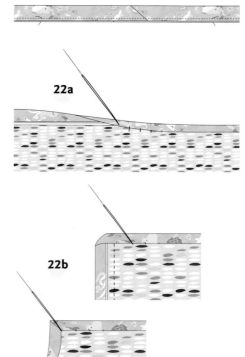

**22** With the back of the quilt facing you and starting on a side, flip the folded edge of the binding to the back of your quilt. Using a hand-stitching needle and sewing thread, stitch the binding to the back of your quilt using a ladder stitch. As you approach the corners, fold the corners into neat miters and sew them in place. When you're done sewing on the binding, trim any loose threads from your quilt. You just completed your quilt—yay!

## FINISH THE PILLOW

**23** Using your rotary cutter, quilting ruler and self-healing cutting mat, trim the excess batting and backing fabric from your pillow top so that the edges line up with the edges of the pillow front. Make sure to keep your corners square.

**24** Cut your pillow envelope fabric to 21½" x 18" (55cm x 46cm). Hem the left 18" (46cm) edge of one of your pillow envelope pieces and the right 18" (46cm) edge of the other. To do this, fold and press the edge over ½"(1cm) and ½" (1cm) again. Then sew the fold with a ¼" (6mm) seam allowance.

**25** Place the envelop pieces on top of the pillow front, right sides together. The raw edges of the envelope pieces should line up with the outer edges of the the pillow front, and the hemmed edges of the envelope pieces will overlap in the center. Sew around the entire edge of the pillow with a ¼" (6mm) seam allowance.

**26** Clip the corners and then turn the pillow right-side out through the opening between the back pieces. Insert a standard-size pillow to complete the project.

**24**

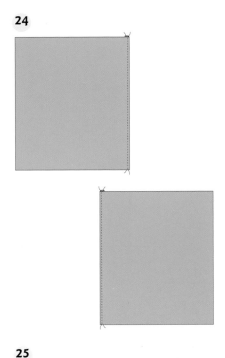

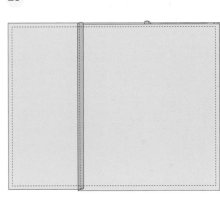

**25**

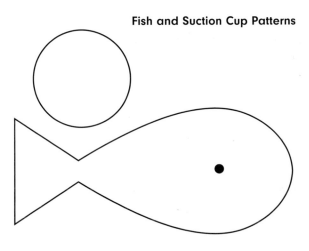

**Fish and Suction Cup Patterns**

# 3 *Just for Fun*

Here at Penguin & Fish, we are all about fun. As a kid, I was constantly pretending and making up stories. My friends and I would put on puppet shows and play games in the backyard, and I could spend hours playing on the couch with my stuffed animals. With the projects in this chapter, I tried to re-create those memories and that sense of play. You'll find some adorable Mini Pets to love and a Barnyard Play Mat for playtime on the go. Send your favorite toy flying with a parachute. See who can hop the fastest in their racing sacks, or write a story and put on a play with the dinosaur Finger Puppets. In this chapter you'll try your hand at cross-stitch, work with felt and burlap, and have fun stitching some silly characters.

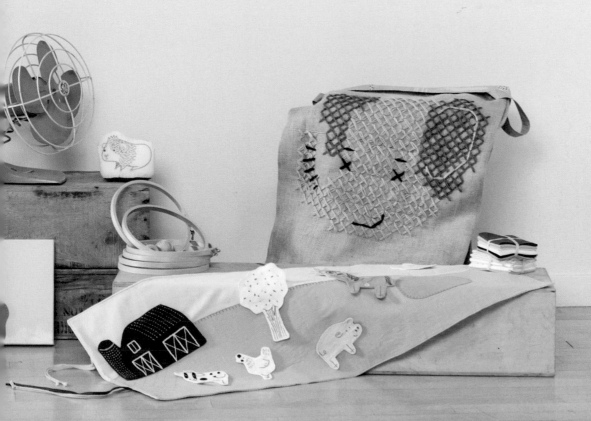

# *Dream Catcher*
## SWEET DREAMS

• Hang this nighttime Dream Catcher on the wall by your bed or from a bedpost. Then let the Dream Catcher's webs capture sweet dreams for you at night (or lovely daydreams for you during the day). The embroidery hoop is used as a frame for the Dream Catcher. Fringed cut feathers hang from strings tied to the hoops. This is a fun project to make, and there's no machine sewing involved.

## Supplies

### EMBROIDERY
- Basic Embroidery Kit (see page 8)
- six-strand embroidery floss (suggested colors: white, yellow, lime green, orange, red, bright blue)
- Sweet Dreams pattern (see Transfer Sheet)
- Feather pattern (see right)

  *choose an 8" (20cm) wooden embroidery hoop with a screw closure (hoop will be used to embroider as well as frame the finished dream catcher)

### FABRIC
- quilt-weight cotton, dark color, for front (embroidery): fat quarter
- quilt-weight cotton for feathers: nine colorful scraps at least 6" x 2½" (15cm x 6cm)

### SEWING, ETC.
- scissors
- hot-glue gun and hot glue

**See page 118 for the Sweet Dreams stitch and color guide**

**Feather Pattern**
Enlarge 200%

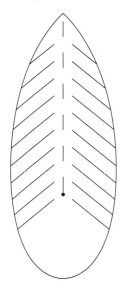

## EMBROIDER THE MOTIF

1  Cut a 12" x 12" (30cm x 30cm) square from the fat quarter. Then transfer the Sweet Dreams pattern to the fabric. (See the transferring techniques on page 16 as needed.)

Place the fabric in the embroidery hoop and, using the floss and needle, embroider your dream catcher. Refer to the stitch and color guide on page 118 for the motif, the stitch library on pages 20–25 and the techniques on pages 18–19 as needed.

## WRAP THE FRAME

**2** Cut three 1½" (4cm) strips lengthwise from your remaining fat quarter fabric. Take your embroidery hoop and loosen the screw closure as far as it will go while still staying attached. Set aside the inner hoop. With your glue gun, tack one end of a fabric strip to the back of the outer hoop close to the closure.

**3** Wrap the strip around the hoop near the closure twice, making sure to keep the strip flat and not twisting it. Continue to wrap around the hoop, covering it. When you reach the end of a strip, tack it in place with the glue gun. Tack down the next strip near the back or inside of the hoop and continue to wrap the hoop with fabric until you've reached the end of the hoop. Wrap the strip around the end of the hoop near the closure twice and then tack it into place toward the back or inside of the hoop. Trim off any excess fabric.

## MAKE THE FEATHERS

**4** Enlarge and transfer the Feather pattern (see page 61) to a piece of scrap fabric. (See the enlarging and transferring techniques on page 16 as needed.) Use that as a template to cut nine feathers from your scrap fabrics and leftover fat quarter. When you are finished cutting, layer the feathers into three sets of three.

**5** With embroidery floss, measure how far from the hoop you would like your feathers to hang. Add extra floss for the length of the feather, plus an additional 6" (15cm). Cut the floss to this length. Repeat for the other two sets of feathers.

**6** Take your first set of feathers and lightly crease the top feather down the center lengthwise. Tie a knot on the end of your first piece of embroidery floss and, using your needle, bring the floss through the first feather from the back to front, starting at the point indicated on the feather template. With a running stitch (see page 21 as needed) and using the crease as a guide, stitch through all the layers of the feather set. Stitch until you've reached the end of the feather. Repeat for the other two sets of feathers.

**7** Hold the long end of the floss against your hoop, letting the feathers hang at the distance where you would like them. Wrap the loose end of the floss around the hoop where you're holding it, making sure to also wrap around the hanging floss near the hoop to hold it in place. Tack the end discreetly with the glue gun to hold it well. Repeat with the other two sets of feathers.

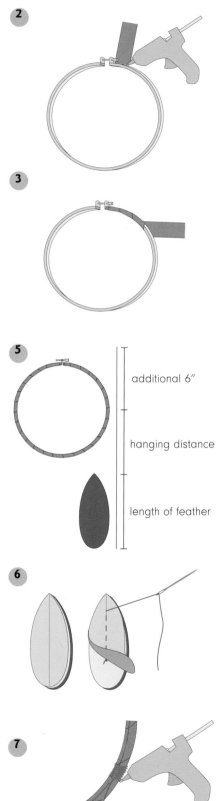

additional 6"

hanging distance

length of feather

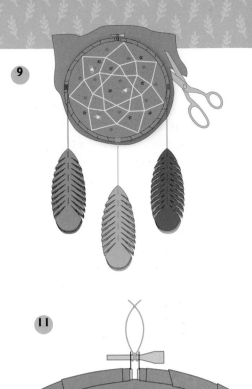

8  Fringe the edges of the feathers by cutting on each side upward diagonally toward the center of the feather, as shown on the Feather template on page 61. Cut through all three layers of fabric. Repeat for the other two sets of feathers.

## ATTACH THE EMBROIDERY

9  Center your embroidery over the inside hoop (which you set aside earlier). Place the outer hoop over the top of the fabric and inner hoop and tighten the closure; pull the fabric taught as you normally would before embroidering. Once your embroidery is secure in your hoop, cut off the excess fabric, leaving ½" (1cm) all the way around.

10  With the glue gun, tack the excess fabric to the inside of the interior embroidery hoop on the back of the dream catcher.

11  Cut 5" (13cm) of embroidery floss and tie it into a loop. Feed it through the embroidery hoop screw closure to make a loop to hang up the finished dream catcher.

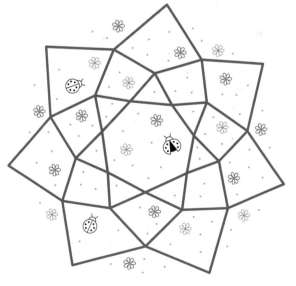

# *Second Stitches*
## DAY DREAMS

● Do you need to take a quick nap? Make sure to have this dream catcher around for lovely day dreams. For this dream catcher (which is pictured on page 60), use cotton quilt-weight fabric in a light color.

**Day Dreams Pattern**
Enlarge 200%
Actual size: 8" x 7.75"
(20cm x 20cm)

**Day Dreams Stitch and Colour Guide**

thick lines: chain stitch • thin lines (bugs): backstitch
dots: French knots • filled-in shapes: satin stitch
• flower petals: lazy-daisy stitch

# Finger Puppets
## T-REX AND TRICERATOPS

SEWING SKILL LEVEL: **1**    EMBROIDERY SKILL LEVEL: **2**

- These wool felt dinosaurs are ready to stomp, stampede and strut! Stitch up a bright gold Triceratops or green T-rex, and your fingers become their legs. This durable and modern take on a classic puppet style is sure to be a hit with the kiddos—and with you! They'd be great for a dino-themed birthday party, or keep them in your purse for playing on-the-go.

## Supplies

### EMBROIDERY

- tear-away, fusible embroidery stabilizer
- pencil or pen (not heat sensitive)
- T-rex and Triceratops patterns (see Transfer Sheet)
- embroidery needle
- embroidery scissors
- six-strand embroidery floss (suggested colors for T-rex: yellow-orange, white, light green, red, black, green; suggested colors for triceratops: purple, yellow, red, black, yellow-orange)

### FABRIC

- wool felt for T-rex: two pieces each 8" x 6" (20cm x 15cm)
- wool felt for Triceratops: two pieces each 8" x 6" (20cm x 15cm)

### SEWING, ETC.

- small, sharp scissors
- iron and ironing board
- light, double-sided, fusible heat-bond adhesive: two pieces (one for each dinosaur): each 8" x 8" (20cm x 20cm)

**See page 118 for T-Rex and Triceratops stitch and color guide**

Note: The instructions below will help you complete one finger puppet. Repeat the steps to make a second puppet.

## EMBROIDER THE MOTIF

1 Using a pencil or pen, trace the dinosaur pattern, including all template markings, to the tear-away fusible embroidery stabilizer. Following the instructions on the package, fuse the stabilizer to the felt.

2 Embroider the motif through the felt and stabilizer using the floss and needle. Refer to the stitch and color guide on page 118 for the motif, the stitch library on pages 20–25 and the techniques on pages 18–19 as needed. Stitch the entire design except for the cut lines (the outermost line around the dinosaur and the circles for the finger holes). Also, make sure your stitches don't cross over the finger holes on the back of your embroidery (because you will be cutting those out).

next step

## ADD THE BACK

**3** From the light, double-sided, fusible heat-bond adhesive, cut a rectangle that is slightly smaller than the embroidered wool felt piece. Follow the adhesive instructions to fuse one side to the second (not embroidered) wool felt piece. Remember to only remove the protective paper from the side that will be fused to your fabric scrap. (Getting the fusible heat bond adhesive directly onto your iron could damage your iron.)

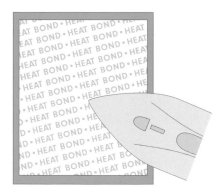

**4** Remove the remaining paper backing from the adhesive. Lay the embroidered felt embroidery side down on the ironing board. With the adhesive side down, place the back wool felt piece on top of the front wool felt piece. Follow the adhesive instructions to fuse the wool felt pieces. Because of the thickness of the felt, you may need to iron for a minute or two.

## FINISH THE PUPPET

**5** With small, sharp scissors, cut out the finger holes through all of the layers. Test the size of the finger holes. If they are too small, trim the edges slightly to make the holes larger.

**6** Cut out the dinosaur along the cut line.

**7** Using the needle and floss, stitch around the finger holes and outer edge using a blanket stitch (see page 24 as needed).

RAR

# Toy Parachute
## OUTER SPACE

SEWING SKILL LEVEL: **2**    EMBROIDERY SKILL LEVEL: **1**

One… two… three… throw! Watch your favorite stuffed animals float to the ground with this fun Toy Parachute. This easy project lets your favorite toy go to outer space with the Martian, rocket ship, Big Dipper and shooting star. Attach a toy and watch it fall in style, or hang it from the ceiling to decorate your room.

## Supplies

### EMBROIDERY
- Basic Embroidery Kit (see page 8)
- six-strand embroidery floss (suggested colors: yellow, orange, white, bright blue, light blue, lime green, red)
- Outer Space pattern (see page 123)

### FABRIC
- quilt-weight cotton, solid color, for the front: 18" x 18" (46cm x 46cm) (cut from ½ yard [46cm] or fat quarter)
- quilt-weight cotton, solid or pattern, for back: 15" x 15" (38cm x 38cm) (cut from ½ yard [46cm] or fat quarter)

### SEWING, ETC.
- Basic Sewing Kit (see page 11)
- water-soluble marker
- yarn (worsted weight): 4½ yards (4.5m)
- chenille needle

**See page 118 for the Outer Space stitch and color guide.**

## EMBROIDER THE MOTIF

1  Enlarge and transfer the Outer Space pattern to your front fabric. (See the enlarging techniques on page 17 and transferring techniques on page 16 as needed.)

2  Place the fabric in the embroidery hoop and, using the floss and needle, embroider your Outer Space motif. Refer to the stitch and color guide on page 118 for the motif, the stitch library on pages 20–25 and the techniques on pages 18–19 as needed.

next step ▸

## SEW THE PARACHUTE

**3** Place the front and back fabrics wrong sides together. Then cut them out along the circle template marks on the front fabric.

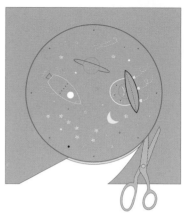

**4** Place the front and back fabric circles rights sides together and pin. Sew around the circle using a ¼" (6mm) seam allowance. Stop about 2½" (6cm) from where you started in order to leave an opening through which to turn the parachute right-side out. Cut notches around the circle in the seam allowance (cutting the notches with pinking shears makes this step super easy). Turn the parachute right-side out through the opening.

**5** Tuck in the raw edges of the opening toward the inside ¼" (6mm) and pin in place, making sure to keep the curve of the edge. Topstitch around the entire edge of the parachute ⅛" (3mm) from the edge, sewing shut the opening in the process.

**6** Cut four 40" (102cm) pieces of yarn. Take one piece of yarn and bring it up through one of the eight template dots around the edge of the parachute, using the needle. Bring the end of the yarn around the edge of the parachute and tie the end to the long end of the yarn with a couple of knots. Take the second end of the yarn and, with the needle, bring it through the template dot immediately next to the dot you just completed. Tie the end the same way as the first end. Repeat this process for the remaining three pieces of yarn and six template dots, creating four loops of yarn on your parachute.

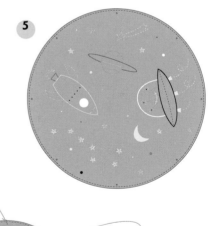

## ATTACH PARACHUTE TO TOY

**7** To attach the parachute to your toy, take all four of the yarn loops in your hand. Wrap the loops around the toy and then pull the parachute through the loops. Drop your parachute from a second-story window or other high place and watch it open.

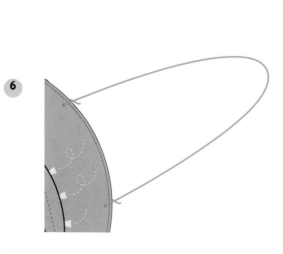

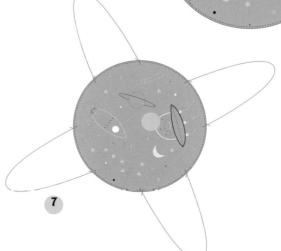

# Second Stitches
## RAINBOW

- Your toy can fly along with a kite, butterflies, hot-air balloon or even a Pegasus with the Rainbow Parachute. Stitch this variation onto a light-colored quilt-weight cotton fabric.

### Rainbow Stitch and Color Guide
thin lines: backstitch
butterfly wings: lazy-daisy stitch
dashed lines: running stitch
thick lines: chain stitch
filled-in shapes: chain stitch
dots: French knot

### Rainbow Pattern
Enlarge 200%
Actual size: 14" x 14"
(36cm x 36cm)

# Mini Pet
## TURTLE

SEWING SKILL LEVEL: **2**     EMBROIDERY SKILL LEVEL: **1**

• Pets are fun! But they can be a lot of work. This almost-life-size pet doesn't need food or a cage—perfect for apartment dwelling. Turtle is sweet, happy and ready to be a wonderful play friend. Colorfully stitched and freestanding, with a cute patterned fabric back, a Mini Pet would look lovely in a kid's room or on a sofa for a bit of whimsy. Change up the colors and make mini portraits of your real-life pet.

## Supplies

### EMBROIDERY

- Basic Embroidery Kit (see page 8)
- six-strand embroidery floss (suggested colors: light green, dark green, gold, red, black)
- Turtle pattern (see Transfer Sheet)

### FABRIC

- quilt-weight cotton fabric, light color, for front (embroidery): 8" x 8" (20cm x 20cm)
- fabric of your choice for back: 8" x 8" (20cm x 20cm)
- fabric of your choice for bottom: 3½" x 8" (9cm x 20cm)

### SEWING, ETC.

- scrap paper
- pen or pencil
- Basic Sewing Kit (see page 11)
- water-soluble marker
- stuffing: small bag (you will have extra left over)

**See page 118 for the Turtle stitch and color guide.**

### EMBROIDER THE MOTIF

1  Transfer the Turtle pattern to your front fabric. (See the transferring techniques on page 16 as needed.) Place the fabric in the embroidery hoop and, using the needle and floss, embroider your motif. Refer to the stitch and color guide on page 118 for the motif, the stitch library on pages 20–25 and the techniques on pages 18–19 as needed.

### CUT THE FRONT AND BACK

2  Using a water-soluble marker and ruler, draw a straight line underneath the embroidered motif from one end to the other. Draw the line 1" (2.5cm) under the embroidery, beginning about 1" (2.5cm) to the left of the embroidery and ending about 1" (2.5cm) past the other edge of the embroidery. This will be the baseline for your mini pet.

3  Continue the line around the entire embroidery 1" (2.5cm) from the embroidery, starting and ending at the baseline. Your start and end points should be at a 90-degree angle.

next step

**4** Layer your front and back fabrics with wrong sides together. Cut through both fabrics along the entire outline.

## CUT THE BASE

**5** From your scrap paper, cut a rectangular strip 3½" (9cm) high with a width at least as long as the baseline of your front fabric. Also cut a piece of thread to the exact length of the baseline.

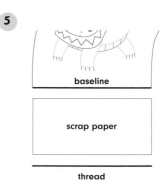

**6** Fold the paper in half lengthwise. Then, using the thread, make an arc on the folded paper, starting and ending on the folded edge with the top of the arch touching the nonfolded edge. Trace the arch with a pencil or pen and cut along the line. Unfold the paper. This will be the template for your pet's bottom.

**7** Using the template you just created, cut out the shape from your bottom fabric.

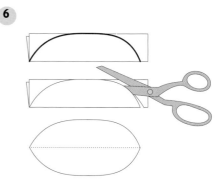

## SEW THE PET

**8** Layer your front (embroidered) and back fabric pieces with right sides together. Pin and machine stitch along the edge with a ¼" (6mm) seam allowance, leaving the baseline unstitched. Cut notches around the curved edges of the seam allowance. Clip into the seam allowance at the valleys.

**9** With right sides together, carefully pin the bottom fabric to the baseline edges of the front and back pieces. Sew around the base with a ¼" (6mm) seam allowance, leaving a 2½" (6cm) opening on the back (with which to turn right-side out). Cut notches around the curved edges of the seam allowance.

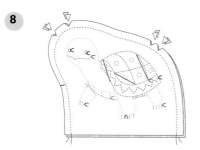

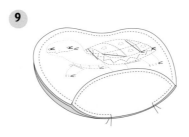

## FINISH STITCHING

10 Turn your mini pet right-side out through the opening at the bottom. With your stuffing, stuff the mini pet through the opening. Don't use large pieces of stuffing. Instead you'll want to stuff little by little to get the stuffing to be even throughout. A chopstick may come in handy to place the stuffing where you would like it.

11 Hand-sew shut the opening using a ladder stitch. (See page 27 as needed.)

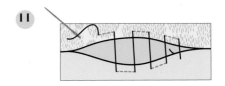

# *Second Stitches*
## PARAKEET AND GUINEA PIG

● Meet Turtle's friends Parakeet and Guinea Pig (shown on page 72). They're ready to come home with you, too!

**Parakeet Pattern**
Enlarge 200%
Actual size: 4.5" x 4" (11cm x 10cm)

**Guinea Pig Pattern**
Enlarge 200%
Actual size: 5" x 3.75" (13cm x 10cm)

**Parakeet Stitch and Color Guide**

lines: backstitch
filled-in shapes: satin stitch

(Yellow represents white floss.)

**Guinea Pig Stitch and Color Guide**

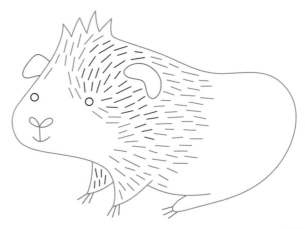

# Play Mat
## BARNYARD DETAILS

- Your little one will be singing "Old MacDonald" all day long with this Barnyard Details Play Mat. The front of the mat is made of flannel that's been appliquéd and embroidered to create a countryside landscape with grassy hills, farm fields and a lake. Use the embroidered flannel barn, horse, chicken, pig and cow play pieces to decorate your scene. When you're done playing, roll up your mat with the pieces and secure it with the colorful ties. You could even pin the mat to the wall; because flannel sticks to flannel, the play pieces will stay in place.

# Supplies

## EMBROIDERY

- Basic Embroidery Kit (see page 8)
- carbon transfer paper
- six-strand embroidery floss (suggested colors: white, light blue, dark red, red, lime green, medium green, golden brown, dark brown, yellow-orange, red-orange, pink, black, teal)

## FABRIC*

- light blue cotton flannel for sky: ½ yard [46cm] (or 42" x 18" [107cm x 46cm])
- green cotton flannel for grass: ½ yard [46cm] (or 42" x 18" [107cm x 46cm])

- blue cotton flannel for lake and tie: ¼ yard [23cm] (or 42" x 9" [107cm x 23cm])
- red cotton flannel for barn and tie: ¼ yard [23cm] (or 42" x 9" [107cm x 23cm])
- white cotton flannel for cow: ¼ yard [23cm] (or 42" x 9" [107cm x 23cm])
- pink cotton flannel for pig, tie: ¼ yard [23cm] (or 42" x 9" [107cm x 23cm])
- cream cotton flannel for chicken: ¼ yard [23cm] (or 42" x 9" [107cm x 23cm])
- light brown cotton flannel for horse: ¼ yard [23cm] (or 42" x 9" [107cm x 23cm])
- light green cotton flannel for tree: ¼ yard [23cm] (or 42" x 9" [107cm x 23cm])
- yellow cotton flannel for tie: ¼ yard [23cm] (or 42" x 9" [107cm x 23cm])
- patterned cotton flannel for backing: ½ yard [46cm] (or 42" x 18" [107cm x 46cm])

  *There will be extra fabric to make multiple play pieces.

## SEWING, ETC.

- rotary cutter
- quilting ruler
- self-healing cutting mat
- Basic Sewing Kit (see page 11)
- double-sided fusible adhesive: 2 yards (1.8m) (assuming 18" [46cm] wide bolt)

**See pages 118-119 for the Barnyard Details stitch and color guide.**

# Play Pieces

Follow steps 1-5 to complete each play piece.

## EMBROIDER THE PIECE

1 From your cotton flannel, cut two pieces that are bigger than the embroidery pattern and will fit in your embroidery hoop. (See the Transfer Sheet for actual size of patterns.)

2 Enlarge and transfer the pattern onto a flannel piece. (See the enlarging techniques on page 17 and transferring techniques on page 16 as needed.) Place the flannel in the embroidery hoop and, using the floss and needle, embroider the design. Refer to the stitch and color guide on pages 118–119 for the motif, the stitch library on pages 20–25 and the techniques on pages 18–19 as needed.

## ASSEMBLE THE PIECE

3 With wrong sides together, cut the two fabric pieces along the cut line on the embroidered front fabric.

4 Pin the pieces with right sides together and sew around the edge, leaving the marked gap open.

5 Turn the piece right-side out through the opening. Then tuck in the raw edges of the opening toward the inside ¼" (6mm) and pin in place. Topstitch around the entire edge of the play piece on the topstitch line, sewing shut the opening in the process.

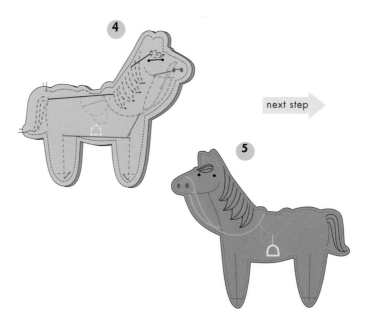

next step

# Play Mat

Follow the remaining steps to complete the play mat.

## ASSEMBLE AND EMBROIDER THE FRONT

**6** Square up the sky, grass and backing fabric together so they are all the same size (approximately 42" x 18" [107cm x 46cm]). Set aside the sky and backing fabric.

**7** With a water-soluble marker, draw a long "S" curve across the grass fabric, about the 10"–12" (25cm–30cm) height of the fabric, to represent hills. Make as many hills as you like. You can draw a straight line if you'd like to create flat plains.

**8** Cut a piece of double-sided fusible adhesive so that it's the length of the grass fabric and larger than the highest point of the "S" curve. Following the instructions, fuse the adhesive to the back of the grass fabric.

**9** If there is any excess adhesive over the edge, trim it off and then cut through the fabric and adhesive along the "S" curve. Take off the paper backing from the adhesive. With the adhesive side facing the front of the sky fabric, place the grass fabric on the sky fabric, aligning the sides and bottom edges. Following the adhesive instructions, fuse the grass fabric to the sky fabric.

**10** Using a water-soluble marker, draw an oval or bean shape on the piece of lake flannel. Then fuse a piece of adhesive to the back of the lake fabric, making sure that the adhesive is slightly larger than the lake outline. Cut through the fabric and adhesive along the lake outline.

**11** Take off the paper backing from the adhesive. With the adhesive side facing the the grass fabric, place the lake fabric where you would like it to be positioned on the grass fabric. Following the adhesive instructions, fuse the lake fabric to the grass fabric.

**12** Hand-stitch along the edges of both the grass "S" curve and the lake with a blanket stitch.

**13** Optional: Embroider a series of diagonal lines on the

**Illustration Color Key**

Light colors represent wrong side; dark colors represent right side.

**7**

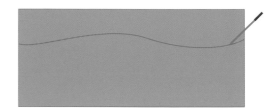

**8**

**9**

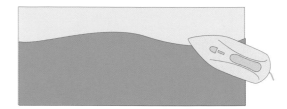

**10**

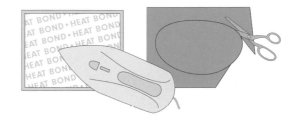

grass, 1" (2.5cm) apart, using a running stitch, to represent the rows in a field. Embroider small vertical stitches in groups of one to three at various points in the grass fabric to represent blades of grass.

## MAKE AND ADD THE FABRIC TIES

**14** Cut a 14" x 1" (36cm x 2.5cm) strip from each of four different colors of the flannel tie pieces. Take the first strip and iron the entire strip in half lengthwise.

**15** Unfold the strip. Fold one of the long edges to the crease and press. Repeat with the other long edge. Then refold the strip along the original lengthwise crease. Sew a line down the length of the tie, securing the folds in place. Tie one of the ends in a knot. Repeat steps 14–15 with the three remaining ties.

**16** Pin the ties onto the front of the mat: Pin two next to each other along the left edge, 5" (13cm) from the bottom of the mat. Match the raw edges of the end of the ties (without the knots) to the edge of the mat. Repeat with the other two ties 5" (13cm) from the top of the mat.

## COMPLETE THE MAT

**17** Pin the mat front and backing fabric with right sides together. Sew around the edges. Start at the bottom edge of the mat and stop about 3" (8cm) from where you began to leave an opening. Clip the corners. Turn the mat right-side out through the opening.

**18** Tuck in the raw edges of the opening toward the inside ¼" (6mm) and pin in place. Topstitch around the edges of the mat with ⅛" (3mm) seam allowance, sewing shut the opening in the process.

Your mat is now complete! To roll up the mat, lay all the play pieces on the mat and then roll up the mat from the right edge. Wrap the ties around the rolled-up mat and tie in a bow.

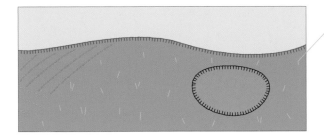

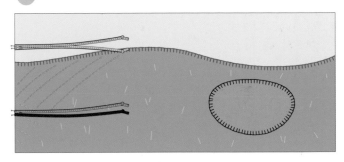

# Racing Sack
## ELEPHANT

- On your mark, get set, go! Who will win? This simple Racing Sack made appropriately from burlap is lined with cotton and includes racing handles. This project gives you a chance to try your hand at cross-stitch, with Elephant created in large, abstract stitches! When you're done racing for the day? Hang the sack on a doorknob and use it to store toys or clothes.

# Supplies

## EMBROIDERY

- pen or pencil (not heat sensitive)
- ruler
- tear-away fusible embroidery stabilizer: at least 20" x 20" (51cm x 51cm)
- tapestry needle
- embroidery scissors
- yarn, worsted weight (suggested colors: light blue, dark blue, red, black, pink)

## FABRIC

- burlap for exterior of sack: 42" x 32" (107cm x 81cm) (1 yard [92cm]) (you may want to purchase a slightly larger piece in order to get clean edges during the fabric prep)
- quilt-weight cotton (cut from ¼ yard [23cm]) for:
  - exterior: 42" x 3¾" (107cm x 10cm)
  - handles: 30" x 4" (76cm x 10cm)
- quilt-weight cotton for lining fabric: 1 yard (92cm)

## SEWING, ETC.

- Basic Sewing Kit (see page 11)
- iron and ironing board

**See page 119 for the Elephant stitch and color guide.**

---

### Illustration Color Key

| exterior burlap fabric | exterior quilting weight fabric | lining fabric |
|---|---|---|
| right side | right side | right side |
| wrong side | wrong side | wrong side |

---

## PREP THE FABRIC

1 To help get rid of messy edges and make sure your burlap is straight, I recommend cutting the burlap along one strand of the weave on each side (following the technique used in the table runner on page 34). Decide where you would like to cut and then snip the burlap ¼" (6mm) in from the edge, next to the strand. Pull the one long burlap strand all the way out of the fabric. This will create a straight line space across the burlap. Cut down the center of that space, which will give you a straight edge. (Repeat for the other edges of the burlap, measuring as you go so you end up with a 42" x 32" (107cm x 81cm) rectangle.

2 Press the burlap over medium heat. Fold the burlap in half along the width of the fabric so you have a 22" x 32" (56cm x 81cm) rectangle. Press, making a crease down the center of the burlap. Open the burlap and lay flat.

## CROSS-STITCH THE MOTIF

3 To make a grid on the burlap and to keep it square and in place while stitching, use tear-away fusible embroidery stabilizer. Cut the stabilizer to a 20" x 20" (51cm x 51cm) square (you may have to lay smaller pieces next to each other to get a 20" x 20" [51cm x 51cm] square). Using a ruler and a pen or pencil, draw a 20" x 20" (51cm x 51cm) grid with cells of 1" (2.5cm) across the square on the nonadhesive side. Mark the center of the grid.

**2**

next step

**4** Lay the grid, adhesive side down, on the burlap, centering it horizontally in the 22" x 32" (56cm x 81cm) rectangle to the right of the crease, and 3½" (9cm) from the top. Following the instructions on the package, fuse the stabilizer to the burlap.

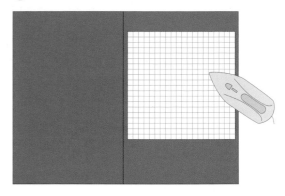

**5** Gently cross-stitch the Elephant motif through the burlap and stabilizer using the yarn and needle. Refer to the stitch and color guide on page 119 for the motif, the cross-stitch instructions on page 25 and the techniques on pages 18–19 as needed. Use the marked center of the pattern and the center of the stabilizer grid as a guide to count the stitches and find where they are located on the grid.

**6** After you're finished with the cross-stitch, carefully tear away the stabilizer. (See page 16 as needed.)

## ASSEMBLE THE SACK

**7** Layer the exterior cotton fabric and burlap with right sides together and matching the 42" (107cm) edge, and pin in place. Sew the pieces together along that 42" (107cm) top edge using a ½" (1cm) seam allowance. Press the seam allowance toward the quilting-weight fabric.

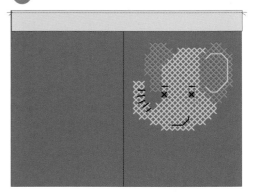

**8** Topstitch along the cotton fabric, ⅛" (3mm) from the seam.

**9** Place the exterior and lining pieces right sides together, matching the edges, and pin. Using a ¼" (6mm) seam allowance, sew the fabrics together along the top edges. Press the seam allowance toward the exterior fabric.

**10** With right sides together, fold the entire piece in half lengthwise, lining up the two long edges. Carefully match up the seams and pin. Using a ½" (1cm) seam allowance, sew along the short, bottom edge of the exterior fabric and along the entire long edge of the two pieces in an "L" shape. Clip the corners on the burlap, then turn the bag right-side out through the opening in the lining fabric.

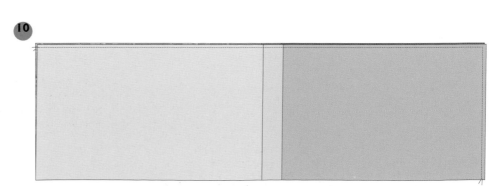

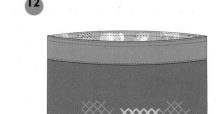

11  Tuck in the raw edge of the lining fabric ½" (1cm) and sew along the opening with a ¼" (6mm) seam allowance, closing the opening.

12  Push the lining into the sack. Sew around the entire opening ¼" (6mm) from the edge. Sew around the opening a second time, ¾" (2cm) from the edge.

## ATTACH THE HANDLES

13  Cut the handle fabric in half so you have two 4" x 15" (10cm x 38cm) strips. Take the first strip and press the short edges over by ½" (1cm) with wrong sides together. Press the entire strip in half lengthwise with the wrong sides together.

14  Unfold the strip lengthwise. With wrong sides together, fold one of the long edges to the crease and press. Repeat with the other long edge.

15  Refold the handle along the original lengthwise crease. Sew around all of the edges using a ⅛" (3mm) seam. Repeat steps 13–15 with the second handle.

16  Pin the handles to the right and left sides of the sack, 1" (2.5cm) from the top, with 4" (10cm) of space between the ends of each handle. Sew the handles in place by first sewing a square attaching each handle end to the sack, then sew an "X" through each square for extra stability.

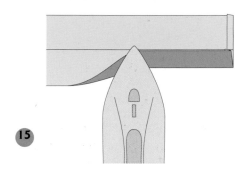

# *Second Stitches*
## LION

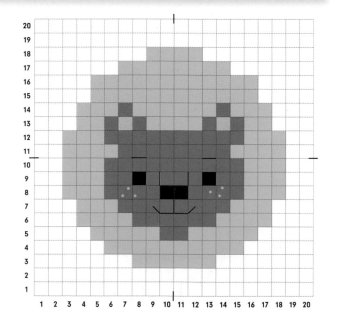

### Lion Color Guide and Cross-Stitch Pattern Chart

- Meet Elephant's racing friend Lion (pictured on page 80). Who will win the race? For the exterior cotton quilt-weight fabric and handles, try a bright red-orange for added color.

# 4 *For Personal Style*

One of the most rewarding things about embroidery is being able to share it with others. There is no better way to do that than to carry it with you! I love personal style projects to wear and hold because they are fun, fashionable and portable. You'll find some lovely projects in this section. Enjoy a shopping day with the Bird-in-Ferns patchwork tote. If you live in Minnesota, like me, or your significant other is in love with the air conditioner, the Upcycled Sweater Scarf will come in handy. Sketch in the park and carry your favorite drawing tools with the Kitty Sketchbook Cover with Pencil Case, and wear your Ladybug Brooch to keep you company. In this chapter, you'll get a chance to use bag-making techniques, learn how to sew with sweaters and find out how to do patchwork without the machine.

# Felt Brooch
## LADYBUG

- Add a cute critter to your wardrobe with this decorative brooch. The Felt Brooch includes a button stitched to the back so it can fit into any open buttonhole on a blouse or coat. Switch out the button for a pin back and you can attach it to a backpack or bag. The Ladybug—as well as spider, grasshopper and butterfly (shown on page 89)—are all smiling and happy to be hitching a ride with you. Make one or a whole swarm.

## Supplies

### EMBROIDERY
- Basic Embroidery Kit (see page 8)
- six-strand embroidery floss (suggested colors: black, red, orange, lime green)
- Ladybug pattern (see Transfer Sheet)

### FABRIC
- quilt-weight cotton for embroidery: 3" x 3" (8cm x 8cm)
- wool felt for front: 4" x 4" (10cm x 10cm)
- wool felt for back: 4" x 4" (10cm x 10cm)

### SEWING, ETC.
- pencil or water-soluble marker
- light, double-sided, fusible heat-bond adhesive: at least 3" x 3" (8cm x 8cm)
- sewing scissors or pinking shears
- button or pin back

**See page 120 for the Ladybug stitch and color guide.**

## PREPARE THE MOTIF

1 Transfer the Ladybug pattern, including the circle, to your cotton fabric. (See the transferring techniques on page 16 as needed.)

2 Follow the fusible heat-bond adhesive instructions to fuse one side to the back of the embroidery fabric. Only remove the protective paper from the side that will be fused to your fabric. (Getting the fusible heat-bond adhesive directly onto your iron could damage your iron.) Carefully cut out the circle.

3 Remove the remaining paper backing from the fusible heat-bond adhesive on your embroidery fabric. Lay and center the embroidery fabric on the front wool felt piece, with the fusible heat-bond adhesive side down. Follow the fusible heat bond adhesive instructions to fuse together the embroidery fabric and front wool felt piece.

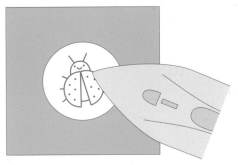

next step

**4** Using a water-soluble marker, draw a circle around the embroidery fabric about ¼" (6mm) away from it.

## EMBROIDER THE MOTIF

**5** Using the floss and needle, embroider your Ladybug motif. Refer to the stitch and color guide on page 120, the stitch library on pages 20–25 and the techniques on pages 18–19 as needed.

## ASSEMBLE THE PIN

**6** Using floss, hand-stitch the button or pin back to the center of the back wool felt piece. Start by bringing up the floss up from the back, through one of the holes on the pin back. Make a couple of small vertical stitches on either side of the hole. Continue in the same manner for the remaining holes.

**7** Pin together the front and back wool pieces, wrong sides together. Be sure to match up the edges of the fabric so that the pin back is centered on the embroidery. (See page 89 if you would like to add leaves.)

**8** Using a blanket stitch, stitch around the embroidery fabric circle through all layers of fabric, securing the back and front wool felt pieces together.

**9** Cut through all the layers of fabric around the outer circle you drew in step 4 on the front wool felt piece. Be careful not to cut through your blanket stitches. For decorative edges, consider using pinking shears instead of standard sewing scissors.

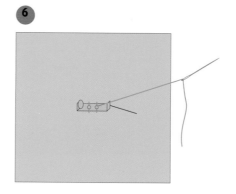

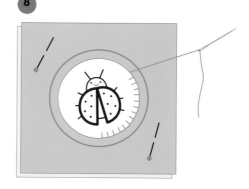

### ADD-ONS: LEAVES

Follow these instructions to add leaves to your pin. After pinning (step 7), cut through all the layers of fabric around the circle on the front wool felt piece. From wool felt scraps, cut out one or two leaves using the leaf template (right) and pin them so they are sandwiched between the circles. Continue with step 8 to complete the button.

**Leaf Template**

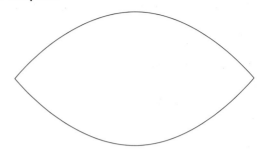

# Second Stitches
## SPIDER, GRASSHOPPER AND BUTTERFLY

- These little critters are ready to crawl, hop and fly into your embroidery hoop! Instead of regular scissors, use pinking shears to fancy up the edges. You can find the patterns for these bug designs on the Transfer Sheet and the stitch and color guides on page 120.

# Drawstring Shoe Bag
## STILETTO

- This linen Drawstring Shoe Bag will protect your shoes in style when traveling or while resting in your closet. Add a pop of color with a bright ribbon for the drawstring and a fun pattern for the lining. This bag is so quick and easy to make, you'll want to make one for every pair of shoes you own. With little adjustments to the embroidery designs, you can make them look like each of your favorite shoes.

## Supplies

### EMBROIDERY
- Basic Embroidery Kit (see page 8)
- six-strand embroidery floss (suggested colors: purple, pink, yellow-gold)
- water-soluble marker
- Stiletto pattern (see Transfer Sheet)

### FABRIC
- quilt-weight cotton or linen, light color, for bag exterior (embroidery): a fat quarter or 18" x 22" (46cm x 56cm)
- quilt-weight cotton for bag lining: a fat quarter or 18" x 22" (46cm x 56cm)

### SEWING, ETC.
- Basic Sewing Kit (see page 11)
- rotary cutter
- quilting ruler
- self-healing cutting mat
- seam ripper
- ribbon, narrow width: 30" x ¼" (76cm x 6mm)
- small safety pin

**See page 120 for Stiletto stitch and color guide**

### Illustration Color Key

| exterior fabric | | lining fabric | |
|---|---|---|---|
| right side | | right side | |
| wrong side | | wrong side | |

## EMBROIDER THE MOTIF

I   Fold the exterior fabric in half lengthwise making a 18" x 11" (46cm x 28cm) rectangle with the fold at the bottom. Mark the center of the 18" x 11" (46cm x 28cm) rectangle using a water-soluble marker. Transfer the embroidery motif to that center. Transfer the Stiletto pattern to that center. (See the transferring techniques on page 16 as needed.) Unfold the fabric.

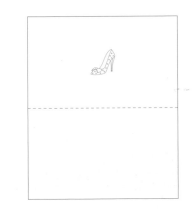

next step

**2** Place the fabric in the embroidery hoop and, using the floss and needle, embroider your Stiletto motif. Refer to the stitch and color guide on page 120, the stitch library on pages 20–25 and the techniques on pages 18–19 as needed.

## SEW THE BAG

**3** Place the lining and exterior bag pieces right sides together and pin. Using a ¼" (6mm) seam allowance, machine sew the fabrics together along the right 22" (56cm) edge. Press the seam allowance toward the exterior fabric.

**4** With the exterior sides together, fold the entire piece in half, lining up the two long edges. Carefully match up the seams and pin. Sew along the short edge of the exterior fabric and the entire long edge of the two pieces in an "L" shape.

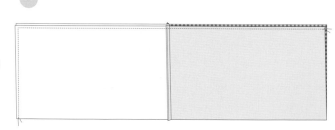

**5** Clip the corners on the exterior fabric and then turn the bag right-side out through the opening in the lining fabric. Tuck in the raw edge of the lining fabric ¼" (6mm) and sew along the opening with a ⅛" (3mm) seam allowance, closing the opening.

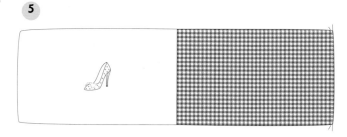

**6** Push the lining into the bag exterior. Pin and topstitch around the entire opening ½" (1cm) from the opening. Sew around the opening a second time, 1¼" (3cm) from the opening.

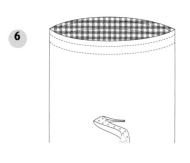

## ADD THE DRAWSTRING

**7** Use a seam ripper to split open the side seam in the space between the two sewn rows at the opening of the bag.

**8** Secure the safety pin to one end of the ribbon. Place the safety pin into the hole at the side seam and use the safety pin to help guide the ribbon the entire length of the opening between the two sewn rows and back out the hole. Tie the ribbon ends in a knot and trim with scissors.

Your shoe drawstring bag is now complete! Close the bag by pulling on the ribbon drawstring.

# Second Stitches
## MEN'S WINGTIP SHOE

- Give your hubby's/boyfriend's/brother's shoes preferential treatment with a bag of their own using the Men's Wingtip Shoe motif, plus darker fabrics and green ribbon. Or try more masculine closures like leather cord or twine.

You can find the Wingtip Shoe pattern on the Transfer Sheet.

**Wingtip Stitch and Color Guide**

thin lines: backstitch
thick lines: chainstitch
French knots: dots

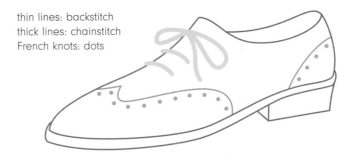

# Upcycled Sweater Scarf
## SNOWFLAKES

SEWING SKILL LEVEL: **2**

EMBROIDERY SKILL LEVEL: **2**

• Made from recycled sweaters on one side and lovely white linen on the other, this beautiful scarf is sure to be your favorite winter accessory. The patchwork squares can be made from several different sweaters to give the scarf different textures and knit designs. The Upcycled Sweater Scarf features subtle embroidered snowflakes on either end and contrasting blanket-stitched edging. This is a quick project, and you'll get a handmade knitted look without the effort of knitting.

## Supplies

### EMBROIDERY

- pen or pencil (not heat sensitive)
- tear-away fusible embroidery stabilizer
- chenille needle
- yarn, worsted weight, same color as your sweaters (see Fabric section) and sparkly (if desired): 1 skein
- six-strand embroidery floss: one skein

### FABRIC

- knit sweaters for the front: 2-5* (depending on the number of textures you want on your scarf)
- linen for the back: ½ yard (46cm) (if the fabric is wider then 63" [160cm], only ¼ yard [23cm] is needed)

*Consider picking up an extra sweater to use for the gloves featured on the next page.

### SEWING, ETC.

- Basic Sewing Kit (see page 11)
- rotary cutter
- quilting ruler
- self-healing cutting mat
- iron and ironing board

**See page 120 for the Snowflakes stitch and color guide**

**Side 1**

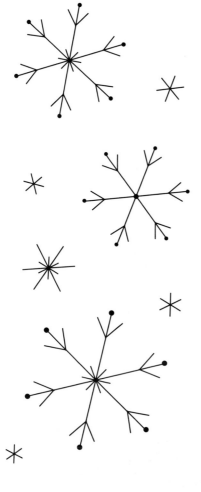

**Side 2**

**Snowflakes Pattern**
Enlarge 250%
Actual size:
Side 1: 5" x 12" (13cm x 30cm)
Side 2: 4.75" x 12.25" (12cm x 31cm)

## PREP THE SWEATERS

1  Wash the knit sweaters following the care instructions on the tags. Using your quilting ruler, self-healing cutting mat and rotary cutter, cut ten 6½" (17cm) squares from the sweaters.

2  With right sides together, carefully pin and sew the sweater squares together in a row using a ¼" (6mm) seam allowance. Try not to stretch the sweaters too much as you sew.

3  Machine stitch around all the edges of the scarf using a ¼" (6mm) seam allowance. This will stop the sweaters from unraveling while you embroider.

## EMBROIDER THE MOTIF

4  Enlarge and transfer the Snowflakes pattern onto the tear-away fusible embroidery stabilizer (see the enlarging and transferring techniques on pages 16 and 17 as needed). Following the instructions, fuse the stabilizer near one short edge of the scarf, about 1" (2.5cm) from the edge. Using the yarn and needle, gently embroider the Snowflake motif on the scarf without pulling or stretching the sweater. (You don't need to use an embroidery hoop because the stabilizer will hold the work in place.) Refer to the stitch and color guide on page 120, the stitch library on pages 20–25 and the techniques on pages 18–19 as needed. After you're finished with the embroidery, carefully tear away the stabilizer.

5  Repeat step 4 to embroider the Snowflake motif on the other end of the scarf. Set aside the scarf front.

## MAKE THE BACK

6  Using your quilting ruler, self-healing cutting mat and rotary cutter, cut two strips from the back fabric that are 6½" (17cm) wide and the length of your fabric. Cut one of the strips in half lengthwise to make two shorter 6½"-wide (17cm-wide) strips. Place the shorter strips on either end of the long strip and sew the three pieces together in a row along the short edges.

**Illustration Color Key**

| | front sweater fabric | | back fabric |
|---|---|---|---|
| right side | | right side | |
| wrong side | | wrong side | |

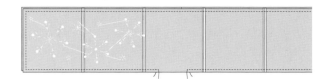

## ASSEMBLE AND FINISH THE SCARF

**7** Measure the scarf front length (it might have stretched a bit while sewing and embroidering). Trim the back fabric strip to the same length.

**8** Place the front and back of the scarf right sides together and pin. Starting in the center along one of the long edges, carefully sew along all the edges. Stop about 3" (8cm) from where you started to leave an opening. Clip the corners and then turn the scarf right-side out through the opening.

**9** Tuck the edges of the opening toward the inside of the scarf. Press and/or pin to hold the edges in place. Using the embroidery floss (do not split the strands), stitch around all the edges of the scarf using a blanket stitch, closing the opening in the process.

**8**

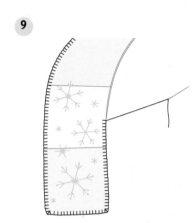

**9**

# *Second Stitches*
## SWEATER MITTENS

- Pick up an extra sweater and fashion yourself a matching pair of mittens for cold climates or chilly cubicles. To find a pattern for sewing mittens (or fingerless mittens like these), simply do an online search for "upcycled sweater mittens"—tutorials abound! Before sewing mittens together, embroider the Snowflake motif to the front of the mittens. Follow the embroidery instructions as you did for the scarf, but transfer only a part of the motif (because the whole motif will not fit). You may also need to shrink the size of the pattern to fit your mittens. Or, if you prefer, try a whole new motif like circles (shown here) or one of your favorite animal friends from another project in this book.

# Tablet Sleeve
## SPOTTED FEATHER

SEWING SKILL LEVEL: **2**   EMBROIDERY SKILL LEVEL: **2**

• This simple, stylish sleeve makes a lovely accessory for any electronic tablet. It's made from two different linen fabrics and is lightly batted to help protect your tablet from bumping around in your bag. On the front is a beautiful and graphic spotted feather made from big satin stitches. This sleeve fits nicely into the Fold-Over Clutch (on page 110).

## Supplies

### EMBROIDERY

• water-soluble marker
• Basic Embroidery Kit (see page 8)
• six-strand embroidery floss (suggested colors: white, black, bright blue)
• Spotted Feather pattern (see Transfer Sheet)

### FABRIC

• linen or quilt-weight cotton, light color (for front/embroidery):  12" x 12" (30cm x 30cm) (cut from ⅓ yard [31cm] or fat quarter)
• linen or quilt-weight cotton in other color for front flap: 3½" x 8¾" (9cm x 22cm)
• linen or quilt-weight cotton in other color (same as above or different) for exterior back: 10¾" x 8¾" (27cm x 22cm) (This and the item above it can be cut from the same ¼ yard [23cm]  or fat quarter)
• linen or quilt-weight cotton for lining: two 10¾" x 8¾" (27cm x 22cm) pieces (cut from ¼ yard [23cm] or fat quarter)
• low-loft batting: two 10¾" x 8¾" (27cm x 22cm) pieces

*The dimensions shown here will make a case perfectly sized for an Apple iPad. You might need to adjust the measurements slightly to fit another brand of tablet.

### SEWING, ETC.

• Basic Sewing Kit (see page 11)
• knitting needle (optional)

**See page 120 for Spotted Feather stitch and color guide**

## EMBROIDER THE MOTIF

1 Using a water-soluble marker, draw a 7¾" x 8¾" (20cm x 22cm) rectangle in the upper right-hand corner of the front fabric. Transfer the Feather pattern to your fabric within the bottom portion of the 7¾" x 8¾" (20cm x 22cm) rectangle. (See the transferring techniques on page 16 as needed.) The Feather motif should be at least 1" (2.5cm) away from the edges of the rectangle.

2 Place the front fabric in the embroidery hoop and, using the floss and needle, embroider your Feather motif. Refer to the stitch and color guide on page 120, the stitch library on pages 20–25 and the techniques on pages 18–19 as needed.

1

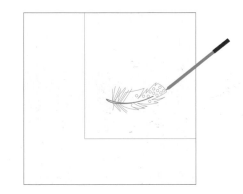

next step

## ASSEMBLE THE BAG

**3** Cut out the embroidered front fabric along the drawn lines of the rectangle.

**4** With right sides together, pin and sew the front flap fabric to the right, 8¾" (22cm) edge of the cream exterior fabric. Press the seam allowance toward the front flap fabric.

**5** Topstitch the front flap fabric ⅛" (3mm) from the seam.

**6** Lay the exterior front, faceup, on top of one of the batting pieces, lining up the edges. With right sides together, place one of the lining pieces on top of the exterior front, lining up the edges. Pin and machine stitch through the layers along the right (top of sleeve) edge. Open up the fabric and press the seam allowance toward the exterior piece. Repeat with the remaining batting, lining and exterior pieces sewing along the left edge instead of the right.

**7** With right sides together, lay the front piece on top of the back piece, matching the front to back and lining to lining. Carefully pin where the seams meet in the center. Both seam allowances should be facing away from the lining pieces. Pin around the remaining edges. Sew around the entire edge starting 2" (5cm) in on the short edge of the lining and ending 2" (5cm) in on the other side of the short edge of the lining, leaving a gap.

**3**
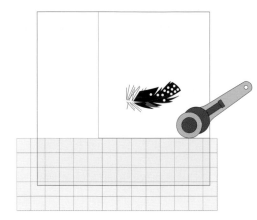

**4**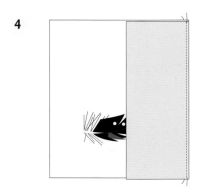

**6**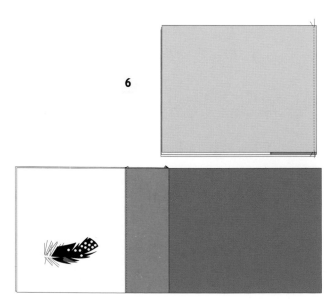

**5**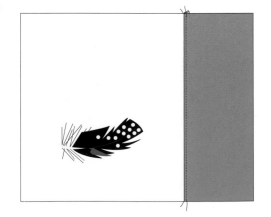

**8** Clip the corners and then turn the sleeve right-side out through the opening in the lining. Push out all of the corners so they are nice and crisp (a knitting needle works great for this). Turn the raw edges of the lining inward ¼" (6mm) and sew shut with ⅛" (3mm) seam allowance.

**9** Push the lining to the inside of the sleeve. Pin and sew around the entire opening ⅛" (3mm) from the opening.

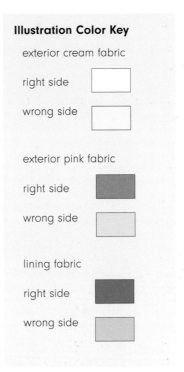

**Illustration Color Key**

exterior cream fabric

right side

wrong side

exterior pink fabric

right side

wrong side

lining fabric

right side

wrong side

**7**

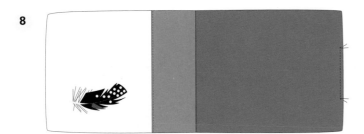

**8**

**9**

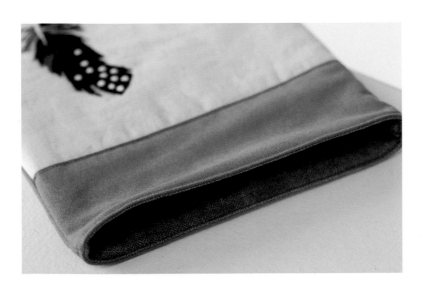

# Sketchbook Cover With Pencil Case
## KITTY & SPEECH BUBBLE

SEWING SKILL LEVEL: **3**

EMBROIDERY SKILL LEVEL: **2**

Cute up your boring black sketchbook with a sketchbook cover that's both functional and fun. This cover has a silly little talking kitty stitched on the front with wool felt and is sure to make you smile. My kitty "Marew"s, but yours could "Mew," "Reow," or "Miau." Your kitty could even say, "Let's Draw." Not only will the sketchbook cover protect your sketchbook from smudges and dings, it also has a zipper pocket on the back to hold your favorite drawing tools.

# Supplies

## EMBROIDERY

- pen or pencil (not heat sensitive)
- tear-away fusible embroidery stabilizer
- scissors
- embroidery needle
- six-strand embroidery floss (suggested colors: black, pink, orange, lime green)
- Kitty & Speech Bubble Pattern (see Transfer Sheet)

## FABRIC

- quilt-weight cotton or linen, light color, for the sketchbook and pencil case exterior: 20" x 9¾" (51cm x 25cm) (cut from ⅓ yard [31cm])
- quilt-weight cotton for pencil case lining: 20" x 9¾" (51cm x 25cm) (cut from ⅓ yard [31cm])
- wool felt scrap for the Kitty: 6" x 4" (15cm x 10cm)
- wool felt scrap for the Speech Bubble: 6" x 4" (15cm x 10cm)

## SEWING, ETC.

- rotary cutter
- quilting ruler
- self-healing cutting mat
- water-soluble marker
- Basic Sewing Kit (see page 11)
- double-sided, fusible heat-bond adhesive (optional)
- zipper foot
- zipper: 7" (18cm) match to Kitty fabric
- ribbon: 8" x ¼" (20cm x 6mm)
- sketchbook: standard 5½" x 8" (14cm x 20cm) hardcover
- iron and ironing board

**See page 121 for Kitty & Speech Bubble stitch and color guide**

## EMBROIDER THE MOTIF

**I** Cut the tear-away fusible embroidery stabilizer into two pieces that measure at least 6" x 4" (15cm x 10cm). Trace the Kitty & Speech Bubble patterns, including all template markings, to the tear-away fusible embroidery stabilizer. Following the instructions on the package, fuse the stabilizer to the Kitty & Speech Bubble felt pieces.

**2** Using the floss and needle, gently embroider the Kitty & Speech Bubble motifs. (You don't need to use an embroidery hoop because the stabilizer will hold the work in place.) Refer to the stitch and color guide on page 121, the stitch library on pages 20–25 and the techniques on pages 18–19 as needed. After you're finished with the embroidery, cut out the kitty and speech bubble along the cut lines. Then carefully tear away the stabilizer.

## CUT THE STRIPS

**3** From the exterior fabric, cut the following strips (all with a height of 9¾" [25cm]): 11¼" (29cm), 7¾" (20cm) and 1" (2.5cm). Turn the 1" (2.5cm) strip 90 degrees and cut two 3½" x 1" (9cm x 2.5cm) pieces. Discard the extra fabric. From the interior fabric cut the following strips (all with a height of 9¾"[25cm]): 19" (48cm), 5½" (14cm), 4" (10cm) and 1¼" (3cm). Discard the extra fabric.

## ATTACH THE KITTY & SPEECH BUBBLE

**4** Lay the 11¼" x 9¾" (29cm x 25cm) exterior fabric piece horizontally on a flat surface. With a water-soluble marker, draw a vertical line 3¼" (8cm) from the right 9¾" (25cm) side. Draw a second vertical line 9" (23cm) from the right side. The space between the lines represents the sketchbook front cover.

**5** Pin the Kitty & Speech Bubble felt pieces where you'd like them on the front cover. (Or, for added security, use double-sided fusible adhesive.) Machine stitch them to the exterior fabric using a ⅛" (3mm) seam allowance, or hand-stitch them using a blanket stitch (see page 24).

next step

## ATTACH THE ZIPPER ENDS

**6** Fold and press the two 3½" x 1" (9cm x 2.5cm) exterior fabric pieces in half with wrong sides together, so the short ends meet. Then open the zipper halfway. Pin together the start of the zipper so the metal stoppers meet. Then place the folded edge of one fabric piece so it overlaps the metal stoppers at the start of your zipper by ¼" (6mm). Pin the fabric in place and sew along the folded edge (right through the zipper) with a ⅛" (3mm) seam allowance, making sure not to sew on top of the metal. Repeat to sew the second piece to the opposite end of the zipper.

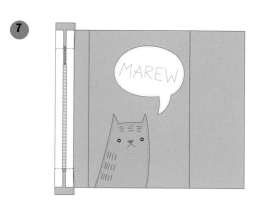

## ASSEMBLE THE PENCIL CASE FRONT

**7** Place the 11¼" x 9¾" (29cm x 25cm) exterior piece on a flat surface, with right side up. With right sides together, place the edge of the zipper tape along the left, short edge of your exterior piece. When closed, the zipper pull should be toward the top edge.

**8** With right sides together, lay the 1¼" x 9¾" (3cm x 25cm) lining piece on top of the exterior piece with the zipper. You should now have the zipper sandwiched between the exterior and interior pieces, with the left edges lined up. Pin in place. Using a zipper foot, sew along the edge about ⅛" (3mm) away from the zipper. When you get to the zipper pull, stop sewing with your needle in the down position and then zip up the zipper. Continue sewing the rest of the edge.

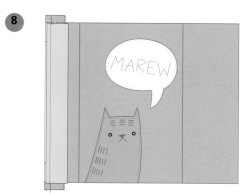

**9** Flip open the exterior piece and the short interior piece so wrong sides are together and the zipper is visible. Press. Topstitch along the zipper ⅛" (3mm) from the seam.

**10** Repeat steps 8 and 9 to sew the exposed zipper edge to the other exterior (7¾" x 9¾" [20cm x 25cm]) and lining (4" x 9¾" [10cm x 25cm]) pieces; the zipper will be sandwiched between the exterior and lining pieces, with right sides together and left edges lined up. Again, sew ⅛" (3mm) away from the zipper.

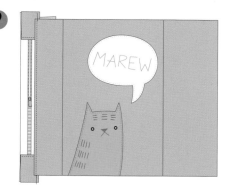

**11** Flip open the second exterior piece and interior pieces so wrong sides are together and the zipper is visible (between the two exterior pieces). Press. Topstitch along the zipper ⅛" (3mm) from the seam (still using the zipper foot). Trim the overhanging edges of the zipper tape flush with the edges of the exterior pieces.

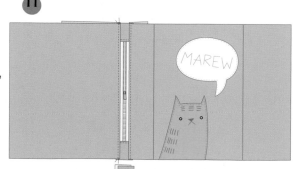

**12** Flip the exterior side over so the wrong side is up and the lining pieces sewn to the zipper are exposed. Lay the pieces flat with their right sides facing up. Take the 5½" x 9¾" (14cm x 25cm) lining piece (the pocket) and, with right sides together, lay it on top of the two attached lining pieces, one on each side of the pocket piece. The long raw edges should line up. Pin and sew along the two 9¾" (25cm) edges, moving the exterior fabric out of the way so you're only sewing the lining fabric pieces.

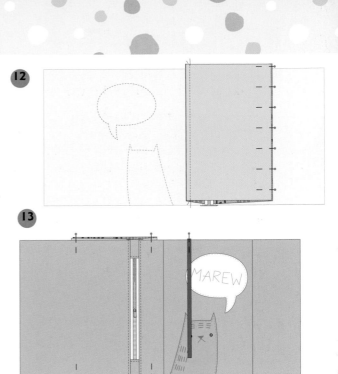

## FINISH THE ASSEMBLY

**13** With the wrong side of the exterior piece still facing up, align and pin the pocket to the top and bottom edge of the exterior fabric so that the pocket lays flat. Flip the exterior piece over so that the right side is facing up. Pin the end of the ribbon to the top edge of the exterior fabric and 7½" (19cm) from the right edge.

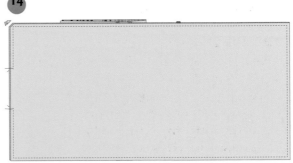

**14** With right sides together, pin the 19" x 9¾" (48cm x 25cm) interior piece to the exterior piece. Sew around the entire pinned edge (also attaching the ribbon and pocket from step 13) with a ¼" (6mm) seam allowance. Leave a 3" (8cm) gap open on the left short edge on the back (or side without the Kitty) of the cover. Clip the corners.

**15** Turn the sketchbook cover right-side out through the opening. Turn the raw edge of the opening inward ¼" (6mm) and pin. Pin and topstitch around the entire edge with a ⅛" (3mm) seam allowance, making sure to move the ribbon bookmark out of the way.

## FINISH THE SKETCHBOOK FLAPS

**16** Set the fabric sketchbook cover facedown and place the closed sketchbook on top of it, making sure that the kitty motif is where you'd like it to sit on the front of the book. With the book closed, fold the overhanging flaps on either side toward the inside cover and pin the flaps in place along the top and bottom edges. Make sure the cover fits well with the book closed, and make any adjustments needed.

**17** Stitch using a ladder stitch (see page 27) the top and bottom edges of the flaps. As an alternative to hand-sewing the flaps, you can machine sew across the top and bottom edges of the flaps with a ⅛" (3mm) seam allowance (but you will need to make sure that your cover is still large enough to have the flap fit with an ⅛" (3mm) seam allowance). Hand-sewing the flaps will ensure a slightly looser fit. Remove any water-soluble marks with a damp cloth.

# Patchwork Tote
## BIRD-IN-FERNS

● This playful Patchwork Tote was inspired by a combination of vintage crewel embroidery and crazy quilting. It features a sweet bird-in-the-ferns motif stitched with yarn and is framed by a scrappy collage of fabrics and decorative stitches. With iron-on adhesive, you get the freedom to play with your fabric scraps and also get a crazy quilt effect without machine sewing the front. The tote is large enough for a quick trip to the grocery store and pretty enough for carrying around town.

# Supplies

## EMBROIDERY

- Basic Embroidery Kit (see page 8) for big stitches

- yarn, worsted weight (suggested colors: orange, brick red, dark brown, olive, light teal, lavender)

- Bird-in-Ferns pattern (see Transfer Sheet)

## FABRIC

- linen, light-colored (for embroidery): 20" x 22" (51cm x 56cm) (cut from ¾ yard [69cm])

- muslin: 20" x 22" (51cm x 56cm) (cut from ¾ yard [69cm])

- six fabric scraps in various colors and patterns: at least 8" x 8" (20cm x 20cm) each

- quilt-weight cotton for back of tote: 1 fat quarter (or 21" x 18" [53cm x 46cm])

- quilt-weight cotton for lining: two pieces, each 15" x 18" (38cm x 46cm) (cut from ½ yard [46cm])

- quilt-weight cotton for handles: two 4" x 20" (10cm x 51cm) strips (cut from 1 fat quarter or ¼ yard [23cm])

## SEWING, ETC.

- water-soluble marker

- light, double-sided, fusible heat-bond adhesive: 1½ yards (1.5m) (assuming a 17"–18" [43cm x 46cm] wide bolt).

- medium, single-sided, fusible interfacing: 15" x 18" (38cm x 46cm) piece

- rotary cutter

- quilting ruler

- self-healing cutting mat

- Basic Sewing Kit (see page 11)

**See page 121 for the Bird-in-Ferns stitch and color guide**

## EMBROIDER THE MOTIF

1  With a water-soluble marker, draw a 15" x 18" (38cm x 46cm) rectangle in the center of your linen fabric. Transfer the Bird-in-Ferns pattern to your fabric. (See the transferring techniques on page 16 as needed.) Center the pattern horizontally within the 15" x 18" (38cm x 46cm) rectangle, and 3¼" from the top of the 15" x 18" (38cm x 46cm) rectangle. Also draw a 15" x 18" rectangle in the center of your muslin. Transfer the oval (not the bird motif) from your pattern. Center the oval as you did on the linen.

2  Place the linen in the embroidery hoop and, using the yarn and needle, embroider the Bird-in-Ferns motif. Refer to the stitch and color guide on page 121, the stitch library on pages 20–25, and techniques on pages 18–19.

## ASSEMBLE THE BAG FRONT

3  From your light, double-sided, fusible heat-bond adhesive, cut a 19" x 21" (48cm x 53cm) rectangle and set aside. Cut your remaining fusible adhesive into pieces that are ¼" (6mm) smaller around all the edges than each of your fabric scraps. Follow your double-sided fusible adhesive instructions to fuse one side to the wrong side of your fabric scraps, centering the adhesive on the scrap. (Iron carefully, as getting the fusible adhesive on your iron could damage it.)

4  Remove the remaining paper backing from the fusible adhesive pieces attached to your fabric scraps. Trim the fabric edges so that the edges are flush to the edge of the adhesive. Slice through your fabric pieces at different angles to create various shapes. Keep your shapes 3"–6" (8cm–15cm) in size.

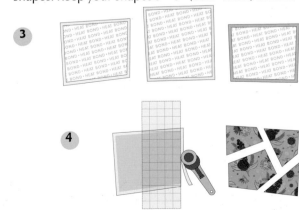

**5** Place your fabric scraps (fabric side up) onto your muslin within the drawn rectangle. Overlap the pieces as desired, making sure to overlap the edges of the 15" x 18" (38cm x 46cm) rectangle and the oval. When you have a collage that you like, follow the fusible adhesive instructions to fuse your fabric collage to your muslin.

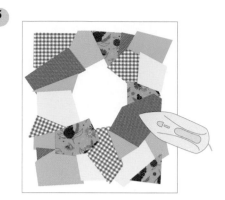

**6** Take the 19" x 21" (48cm x 53cm) fusible adhesive piece, and fuse it to the back of your muslin-and-fabric-collaged piece, centering the adhesive.

**7** Flip your muslin over so the collage side is up. With a water-soluble marker, redraw the 15" x 18" (38cm x 46cm) rectangle and oval (from the pattern). Remove the paper backing from the fusible adhesive. Cut out your 15" x 18" rectangle with the rotary cutter, and then carefully cut out the oval with sharp fabric scissors.

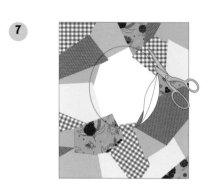

**8** Place your embroidered linen fabric, embroidery side up, on a flat ironable surface. With the fusible adhesive side down, lay your collaged fabric piece on top of the embroidered fabric. Match up the ovals so that the collaged oval frames the embroidery. Iron the collaged fabric to your embroidered fabric, starting at the edge of the oval and working your way outward. Because of all the fabric layers, you may have to press each area for 30 seconds or more. Avoid ironing the embroidery stitches.

**9** Using floss, embellish your tote front with decorative stitches, stitching through all the layers of fabric. I stitched around the oval with a blanket stitch (see page 24) and stitched along every collaged fabric edge with other decorative stitches (see page 23). You don't need to embroider the outer edge of the rectangle.

**10** Following the fusible interface instructions, iron your single-sided fusible interface to the wrong side of your tote back fabric. Trim the back fabric to the 15" x 18" (38cm x 46cm) fusible interface.

## SEW THE TOTE

**11** With right sides and top edges together, sew one of the lining fabrics to the tote front along the top edge with a ¼" (6mm) seam allowance. Flip your fabric open and press flat with the seam allowance going towards the tote front. Your seam will be bulky and facing away from the lining. Repeat with the other lining piece and back of the tote.

**12** With right sides together, lay the front-and-lining piece on top of the back-and-lining piece, matching the front to back and lining to lining. Carefully pin where the seams meet in the center. Both seam allowances should be facing away from the lining pieces. Pin around the remaining edges. Sew around the entire edge, starting 2" (5cm) in on the short edge of the lining and ending 2" (5cm) in on the other side of the short edge of the lining.

13 To remove some bulk from the seam allowance, cut an arc near the seam where the lining meets the exterior of the tote.

14 Cut a 1¼" (3cm) square from one of the tote corners.

15 Separate the layers of the corner, matching up the side and bottom seams. Pin the edge with the seams open. Stitch across the raw edge with a ¼" (6mm) seam allowance. Repeat steps 14 and 15 with the remaining three corners.

16 Turn the entire tote right-side out through the opening in the lining. Use your hand to push out all of the corners. Turn the opening edges of the lining inward ¼" (6mm) and sew shut.

17 Push the lining to the inside of your tote. Topstitch all the way around the top edge of your tote ¼" (6mm) from the top. Repeat at ½" (1cm) from the top of the tote to create two rows of topstitching.

## ADD THE HANDLES

18 Take one handle piece and press the short edges over by ½" (1cm) with wrong sides together. Press the entire strip in half lengthwise with the wrong sides together.

19 Unfold the strip lengthwise. With wrong sides together, fold one of the long edges to the crease and press. Repeat with the other long edge.

20 Refold the handle along the original lengthwise crease. Sew along each of the long edges with a ⅛" (3mm) seam. Repeat steps 18–20 with the second handle.

21 Pin the handles to your tote 4½" (11cm) from the sides and 1" (2.5cm) from the top of your tote. Sew the handles in place by first sewing a square attaching each handle end to the tote, then sew an "X" through each square for extra stability.

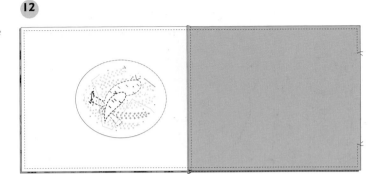

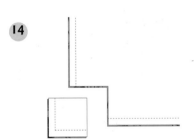

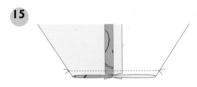

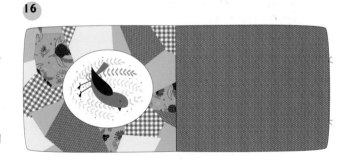

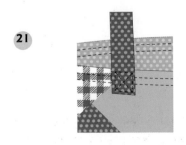

# Fold-Over Clutch
## FEATHER

- This slouchy, oversized Fold-Over Clutch is stylish as well as functional. The beautiful satin-stitched feather on the front is fun to embroider and looks artsy and organic when it's finished. The clutch's fold-over design is roomy enough to fit a tablet or book, cell phone and a few daily accessories. And it features an interior pocket and an optional removable shoulder strap. Pair this project with the Tablet Sleeve (on page 98) for perfect coordination.

**Illustration Color Key**

| exterior cream fabric | | exterior pink fabric | | lining fabric | |
|---|---|---|---|---|---|
| right side | | right side | | right side | |
| wrong side | | wrong side | | wrong side | |

# Supplies

## EMBROIDERY

- Basic Embroidery Kit (see page 8)
- six-strand embroidery floss (suggested colors: white, black, bright blue)
- Feather pattern (see Transfer Sheet)

## FABRIC

- linen or quilt-weight cotton, light color, for exterior front (embroidery): 16" x 12" (41cm x 30cm) (cut from ⅓ yard [31cm] or fat quarter)
- linen or quilt-weight cotton in second color for:
    exterior front panel: 12½" x 4½" (32cm x 11cm)
    exterior back: 12½" x 12½" (32cm x 32cm)
    pocket lining: 7½" x 4½" (19cm x 11cm)
    zipper ends: two 4" x 1½" (10cm x 4cm) pieces
    D-ring tabs (optional): two 3" x 3" (8cm x 8cm) pieces (cut from ½ yard [46cm] total)
- linen or quilt-weight cotton in third color for:
    lining: two 12½" x 12½" (32cm x 32cm) squares
    pocket: 7½" x 4½" (19cm x 11cm) (need ½ yard [46cm] total)
- linen or quilt-weight cotton for strap (optional): 3" (8cm) x width of fabric (assuming at least a 42" [107cm] bolt)

## SEWING, ETC.

- Basic Sewing Kit (see page 11)
- rotary cutter
- quilting ruler
- self-healing cutting mat
- sewing machine zipper foot
- zipper: 12" (30cm)
- low-loft batting: two 12½" x 12½" (32cm x 32cm) squares
- two metal D-rings (optional): ¾" (2cm)
- two metal swivel latches for strap (optional): ¾" (2cm)
- cardboard scrap: 4" x 4" (10cm x 10cm)
- two jump rings (found in jewelry section): ¼" (6mm) or slightly larger
- pliers

**See page 121 for Feather stitch and color guide**

## EMBROIDER THE MOTIF

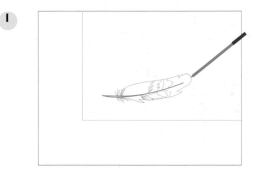

1 With the exterior front/embroidery fabric placed horizontally, and using a water-soluble marker, draw a horizontal 12½" x 8½" (32cm x 22cm) rectangle in the upper right-hand corner on the fabric. Transfer the Feather pattern to the fabric within the bottom-left portion of the rectangle. (See the transferring techniques on page 16 as needed.) The feather should be at least 1" (2.5cm) away from the edges of the rectangle.

2 Place the fabric in the embroidery hoop and, using the floss and needle, embroider your Feather motif. Refer to the stitch and color guide on page 121, the stitch library on pages 20–25 and the techniques on pages 18–19 as needed.

## ASSEMBLE THE CLUTCH FRONT

3 Cut out the exterior fabric along the 12½" x 8½" (32cm x 22cm) rectangle lines. Sew the 12½" x 4½" (32cm x 11cm) exterior front panel piece to the top of the 12½" x 8½" (32cm x 22cm) embroidered fabric with a ¼" (6mm) seam allowance. Press the seam allowance toward the panel. Topstitch on the panel fabric ⅛" (3mm) from the seam. Set aside.

next step

## ADD THE D-RING TABS (OPTIONAL)

(Note: You can choose for your clutch to be just a clutch or to include a detachable shoulder strap. If you choose to add the strap (see steps 19-23), you will need to add the D-ring tabs. If not, you can skip to step 6.)

**4** To make fabric tabs for the D-rings, take one of the 3" x 3" (8cm x 8cm) fabric squares for the D-ring tabs, fold it in half with wrong sides together and press. Unfold the pieces and, with wrong sides together, fold one of the edges to the crease and press. Repeat with the opposite edge. Refold the fabric along the original crease. Sew along the folded edges with a ⅛" (3mm) seam. Repeat with the second fabric square.

**5** Put your new fabric tab through the D-ring and fold the tab in half around the straight edge of the D-ring. Pin the ends together. Repeat with the second tab. Pin your D-ring tabs to the front exterior piece, one along each of the sides, directly below the seam where the two front fabrics meet. Place the D-ring tab so it overlaps the front exterior fabric ¾" (2cm), letting the raw end hang over the side of the exterior fabric. Tack the D-ring tabs in place onto the exterior fabric by sewing with a ⅛" (3mm) seam allowance. Set aside.

## MAKE THE INTERIOR POCKET

**6** Place the two pocket fabrics right sides together and pin. Sew around the pocket leaving 2" (5cm) open along one of the long edges. Clip the corners, then turn right-side out through the opening.

**7** Topstitch along the long edge opposite the opening. Tuck in the raw edges of the opening toward the inside ¼" (6mm) and pin in place.

**8** On the right side of one of the lining fabric pieces, place and pin the pocket (pocket lining side facing the clutch lining fabric piece) with the top stitched edge of the pocket 6" (15cm) from the bottom of the lining piece. With a ⅛" (3mm) seam allowance, sew the pocket along the sides and the bottom, closing the raw edge of the pocket opening in the process. Sew back and forth several times at the beginning and end to reinforce the pocket opening.

## PREP THE ZIPPER

**9** Press the zipper tape flat. To shorten the zipper from 12" (30cm) to 11" (28cm), first measure and mark the zipper at the 11" (28cm) point (measure the actual zipper length and not the entire zipper tape). Tack the zipper at the 11" (28cm) mark by backstitching right over the zipper tape. Cut off the zipper ½" (1cm) beyond the tacking stitches.

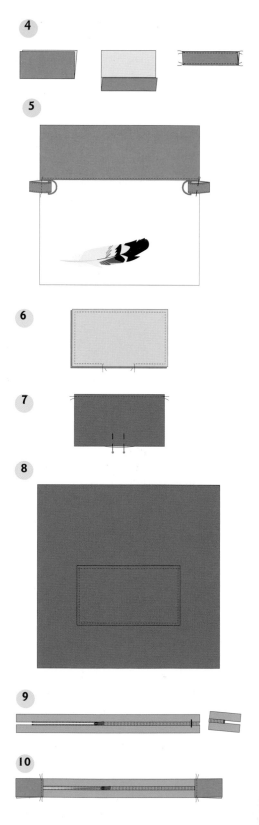

**10** Take the two 4" x 1½" (10cm x 4cm) zipper end pieces and fold each in half so the short ends meet. Press. Open the zipper halfway. Pin together the start of the zipper so the metal stoppers meet. Place the folded edge of one of the fabric pieces so it overlaps the metal stoppers at the start of your zipper by ¼" (6mm). Pin the fabric in place and sew along the folded edge (right through the zipper) with a ⅛" (3mm) seam allowance, making sure not to sew on top of the metal. Repeat to sew the second piece to the opposite end of the zipper overlapping the sewn tack.

## ASSEMBLE THE BAG

**11** Lay your batting and front exterior piece in front of you with the front exterior piece facing up on top of the batting. With right sides together, place the edge of your zipper tape along the top edge of your front exterior piece, centering the zipper along the edge.

**12** Next, with right sides together, lay the lining piece without the pocket on top of the front exterior piece. You should now have your front exterior piece and a lining piece with the zipper sandwiched between them, all with the top edges lined up. Pin the top edge in place. Using a zipper foot, sew along the pinned edge ⅛" (3mm) away from the zipper. When you reach the zipper pull, stop sewing with your needle in the down position, then zip up the zipper so it's out of your way. Continue sewing the rest of the edge.

**13** Flip open the front exterior piece and the lining so wrong sides are together and the zipper is visible. Press. Topstitch along the zipper ⅛" (3mm) from the seam (still using the zipper foot).

**14** Lay the remaining lining piece in front of you facing up. Place the exposed zipper tape along the top edge of the lining piece with the zipper and front exterior piece facing up. With right sides together, take your back exterior piece and align the top edge with the top edge of the lining and zipper tape. The zipper will be sandwiched between the back exterior piece and remaining lining piece, with top edges lined up. Using the zipper foot, sew ⅛" (3mm) away from the zipper.

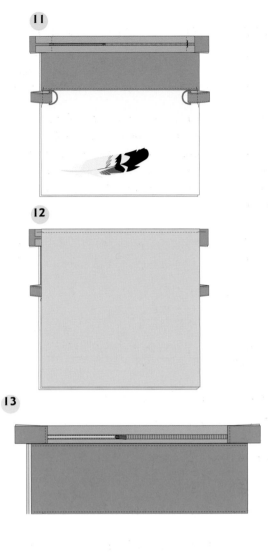

**11**

**12**

**13**

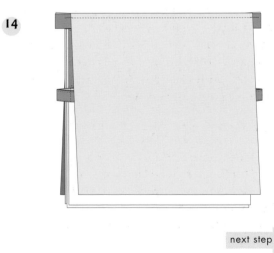

**14**

next step ▶

**15** Flip open the back exterior piece and the lining so wrong sides are together and the zipper is exposed in the middle of the two fabrics. Press. Topstitch along the zipper ⅛" (3mm) from the seam (still using the zipper foot). Trim flush the overhanging edges of the zipper end fabric.

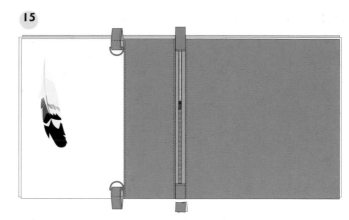

**16** Open your zipper all the way. (Don't skip this part!) Flip open your fabric pieces and align them so the right sides of the exterior pieces are facing each other and the right sides of the lining pieces are facing each other. Pin along the entire outside edge. When you get to the middle where your zipper ends are, fold the zipper ends so that the fold is directed toward the lining pieces. It will be a bit bulky here.

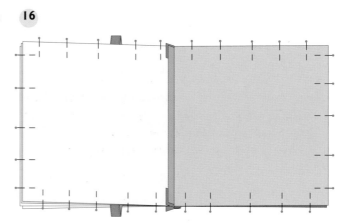

**17** Sew around all the edges using a ¼" (6mm) seam allowance, leaving a 5" (13cm) opening at the base of the lining. Clip the corners.

**18** Turn the clutch right-side out through the opening in the lining. Turn the raw edge of the opening in the lining inward ¼" (6mm) and sew shut. Push the lining to the inside of your clutch.

## MAKE THE STRAP (OPTIONAL)

(Note: Complete this section only if you added the D-ring tabs earlier in step 4. If you are not adding a strap, skip to step 24.)

**19** On the strap fabric, fold and press both short ends ½" (1cm) (right sides together). Then fold and press the fabric in half lengthwise.

**20** Unfold the strip. Fold one of the long edges to the crease and press. Repeat with the other long edge.

**21** Refold the strip along the original lengthwise crease. Sew around all of the edges with a ⅛" (3mm) seam allowance.

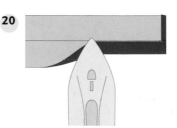

**22** Loop either end of the strap through a swivel latch and pin the end to the strap. Adjust and repin the length of the loops until you reach your desired strap length.

**23** Sew a square attaching the strap end to the strap, then sew an "X" through the square for extra stability. Repeat with the other end of the strap. For additional support, sew a straight stitch through the strap loops ¾" (2cm) from the swivel latches.

## ADD THE ZIPPER-PULL TASSEL

**24** Wrap the zipper-pull floss around the 4" x 4" (10cm x 10cm) cardboard scrap 15–20 times, ending on the same end that you started with. Trim the end of the floss, leaving about a 12" (30cm) tail.

**25** Open one of the jump rings. Carefully take the embroidery floss off of the cardboard and place the loop on top through the jump ring. Cut off the loop on the bottom so the ends hang straight to your desired tassel length. Be sure not the cut the 12" (30cm) tail short. Close the jump ring using the pliers.

**26** Pinch the tassel between your fingers right under the jump ring. Take the 12" (30cm) tail and wrap it tightly around the tassel loops, starting about ½" (2cm) from the jump ring and working toward the jump ring. Stop wrapping about ¼" (6mm) from the jump ring.

**27** Thread the end of the tail through the needle. Insert your needle through the center of the loops you just made by wrapping to the bottom of the wrapping. Pull tight. Trim the tail to the length of the tassel.

**28** Open the second jump ring and hook it through the tassel jump ring and the hole in the zipper pull. Close the jump ring with your pliers.

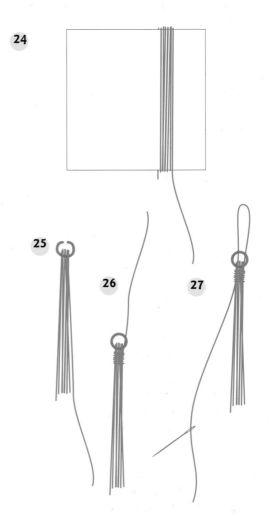

# Stitch and Color Guides
## CHAPTER 2 GUIDES

Unless otherwise noted,
use the following stitches:
lines: backstitch
filled-in shapes: satin stitch
dots: French knot
dashed lines: running stitch
"X"s: cross-stitch

Queen Anne's Lace
leaves

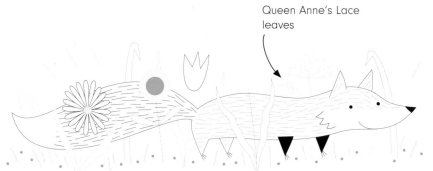

**Fox & Flowers**
(Table Runner, page 34)

Queen Anne's lace: feather stitch

Blue represents white floss.

**"What a Lovely Evening" Owl**
(Wall Art, page 30)

lines for branches: stem stitch
wings: long and short stitch
leaves: single chain stitch
feathers: fly stitch

**Woodland Creatures**
(Coffee Cozy, page 36)

leaves: single chain stitch
flowers: lazy-daisy stitch

For the bow, first stitch the
line with a backstitch. Next,
bring the needle up at the
end of a bow string, then
weave in and out of the
backstitch. Repeat, weaving
in the opposite direction.

**Barn Owl**
(Throw Pillow,
page 44)

thin lines (face):
backstitch
face: short and
long stitch
feathers: fly stitch
thick lines (owl
outline): chain
stitch

Light blue
represents white
floss.

**Skunk**
(Floor Pillow,
page 40)

Yellow represents
white floss.

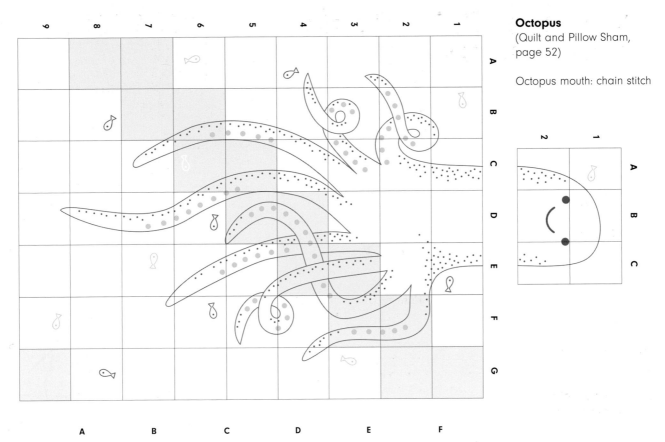

**Octopus**
(Quilt and Pillow Sham, page 52)

Octopus mouth: chain stitch

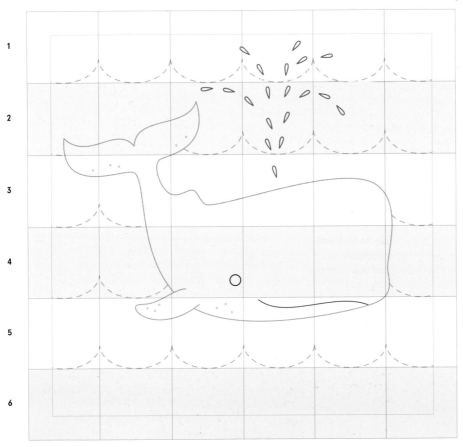

**Whale**
(Shower Curtain, page 48)

water spout droplets: single chain stitch

# Chapter 3 Guides

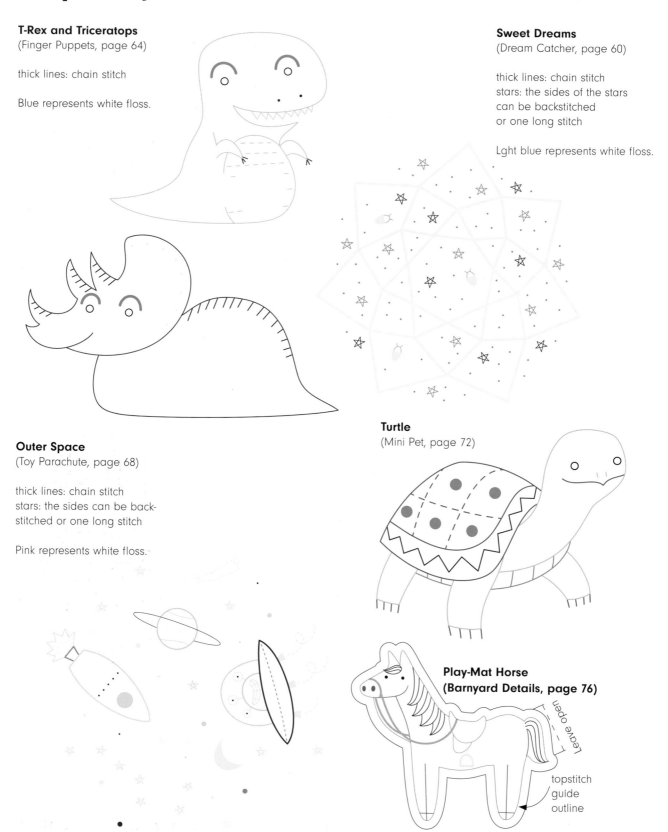

**T-Rex and Triceratops**
(Finger Puppets, page 64)

thick lines: chain stitch

Blue represents white floss.

**Sweet Dreams**
(Dream Catcher, page 60)

thick lines: chain stitch
stars: the sides of the stars
can be backstitched
or one long stitch

Lght blue represents white floss.

**Outer Space**
(Toy Parachute, page 68)

thick lines: chain stitch
stars: the sides can be backstitched or one long stitch

Pink represents white floss.

**Turtle**
(Mini Pet, page 72)

**Play-Mat Horse**
(Barnyard Details, page 76)

Leave open

topstitch
guide
outline

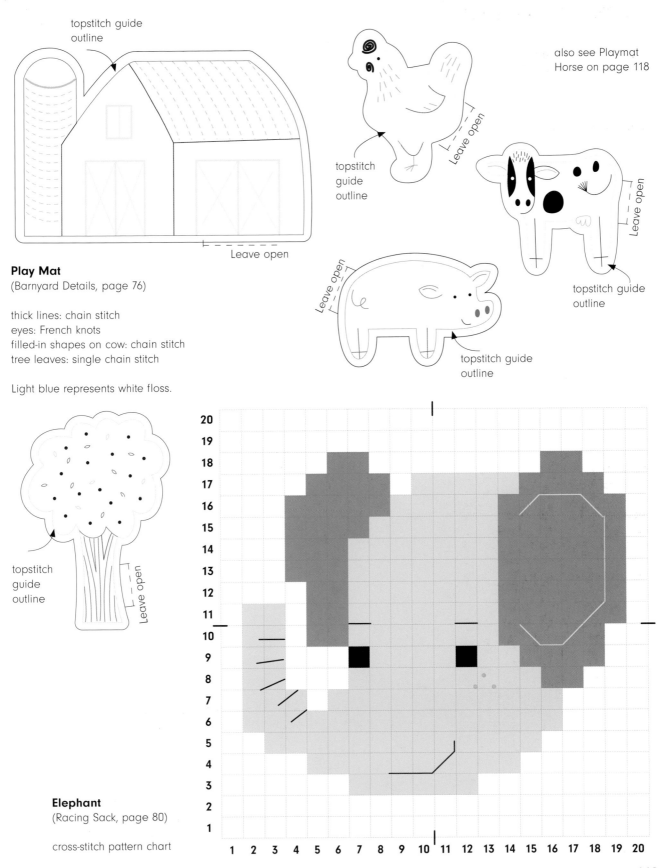

topstitch guide outline

Leave open

also see Playmat Horse on page 118

topstitch guide outline

Leave open

Leave open

topstitch guide outline

topstitch guide outline

**Play Mat**
(Barnyard Details, page 76)

thick lines: chain stitch
eyes: French knots
filled-in shapes on cow: chain stitch
tree leaves: single chain stitch

Light blue represents white floss.

topstitch guide outline

Leave open

**Elephant**
(Racing Sack, page 80)

cross-stitch pattern chart

20
19
18
17
16
15
14
13
12
11
10
9
8
7
6
5
4
3
2
1

1  2  3  4  5  6  7  8  9  10  11  12  13  14  15  16  17  18  19  20

# Chapter 4 Guides

side 1

side 2

**Snowflakes**
(Upcycled Sweater Scarf, page 94)

Lines can be backstitched or one long stitch.

Light blue represents white floss.

**Stiletto**
(Drawstring Shoe Bag, page 90)

**Felt Brooches**
(Ladybug, Grasshopper, Butterfly, Spider, page 86)

thick lines on Ladybug: chain stitch

**Spotted Feather**
(Tablet Sleeve, page 98)

Feather shaft: stem stitch
Feather down lines: backstitch or one long stitch

Light blue represents white floss.

feather shaft

feather down lines

**Kitty & Speech Bubble**
(Sketchbook Cover With Pencil Case, page 102)

stripes: can be backstitched or one long stitch

Cut lines
(do not stitch)

**Feather**
(Fold-Over Clutch, page 110)

feather shaft: stem stitch
feather down lines: backstitch or one long stitch

Light blue represents white floss.

feather shaft

Feather
down lines

**Bird-in-Ferns**
(Patchwork Tote, page 106)

filled-in shapes: long and short stitch
leaves: lazy-daisy stitch

**Piece 1**

**Barn Owl
Pattern**
Enlarge 200%
Actual size: 12" x
12" (30cm 30cm)

**Fox & Flowers Pattern**
Enlarge 200% (then tape the two pieces of the pattern together where they match up)

**Piece 2**

**Outer Space Pattern**
Enlarge 250%
Actual size: 14" x 14 "
(36cm x 36cm)

# Resources

## DMC

dmc-usa.com
embroidery floss (six-strand and Perle), needles, water-soluble marker

## Cosmo

lecienusa.com/shop/category/thread/
embroidery floss

## Clothworks Textiles

clothworkstextiles.com
manufacturer of Penguin & Fish organic quilt-weight cotton fabric

## Spoonflower

spoonflower.com
Create your own custom printed fabric.

## National Nonwovens

commonwealthfelt.com
100% wool craft felt

## FriXion Pen

pilotpen.us/Brands/FriXion.aspx
heat-sensitive ink pen

## Sulky

sulky.com
iron-on transfer pen, embroidery stabilizer

## Pellon

pellonideas.com
double-sided fusible adhesive, interfacing, embroidery stabilizer

## Gingher

gingher.com
scissors, embroidery scissors, pinking shears

## Saral Paper Corp.

saralpaper.com
graphite transfer paper

# About the Transfer Sheet

The pull-out Transfer Sheet accompanying this book includes full-size patterns for 11 of the projects in this book.

**How to use:** For the pattern you would like to use, first cut out the pattern from the sheet. Cover your ironing board with paper towels or a paper bag to protect it from bleeding ink. Preheat your fabric by ironing where you would like the design to be. Lay the pattern, ink side down, onto your fabric. Hold the iron on the back of the pattern for about 10 seconds. Check a corner to see if the pattern has transferred completely, then peel away. Note: Your transfer will be permanent. Take care not to move the pattern when you iron.

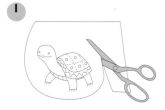

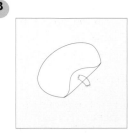

# Index

# *Acknowledgments*

# *Dedication*

For my mom and grandma.

Many awesome thanks to:

Jon, for being my wonderful husband and champion in creating this book.

My mom, for her love, support, patience and amazing sewing abilities.

My dad, for his logistical support, i.e., the drinks and eats for our many sewing sessions in Fond du Lac, Wisconsin.

Sarah Hebenstreit, for her incredible photographic eye and easy collaboration on this book.

Our lovely cover model, Annie, and our super duper kid models, Luca, Marley, Lucas and Elliana. All y'all were amazing!

Kristin, my editor, and Pru, my designer, for all their fantastic work. Thanks so much!

The folks at Clothworks Textiles, for making my designs into beautiful lines of organic fabric.

www.fwmedia.com

17   16   15   14   13      5   4   3   2   1

Distributed in Canada by Fraser Direct
100 Armstrong Avenue
Georgetown, ON, Canada  L7G 5S4
Tel: (905) 877-4411

Distributed in the U.K. and Europe by F&W MEDIA INTERNATIONAL
Brunel House, Newton Abbot, Devon, TQ12 4PU, England
Tel: (+44) 1626 323200, Fax: (+44) 1626 323319
Email: enquiries@fwmedia.com

Distributed in Australia by Capricorn Link
P.O. Box 704, S. Windsor NSW, 2756 Australia
Tel: (02) 4577-3555

SRN: V9284
ISBN-13: 978-1-44023263-3

Edited by Kristin Boys
Designed by Prudence Rogers
Production coordinated by Greg Nock
Photography by Sarah Hebenstreit
Styling by Lisa Moir
Hair & Makeup by Tricia Turner

# About the Author

Alyssa Thomas is an illustrator, designer and artist. As a child, Alyssa would make everything from beaded bracelets to large papier maché masks and then barter them with her brothers at the "trading post" outside her bedroom door.

Alyssa earned a Bachelor of Fine Arts degree from the Minneapolis College of Art & Design. Alyssa works as a product designer for children's apparel and the stationery industry and illustrated her first children's picture book, No Monster Here.

Alyssa founded Penguin & Fish to create lovely and quirky hand embroidery patterns, embroidery kits, sewing patterns and artful plush. Penguin & Fish's products can be found in quilting, sewing, and gift stores worldwide and at www.penguinandfish.com.

Alyssa blogs at penguinandfish.blogspot.com and tweets under the handle @penguinandfish.

# Take Your Stitching to the Next Level!

### The Stitch Bible

A Comprehensive Guide to 225 Embroidery Stitches and Techniques
Kate Haxell
In this comprehensive guide to embroidery, readers will learn the basic stitches and master eight different embroidery styles, including blackwork, crewelwork, hardanger, pulled thread, goldwork and freestyle. Every stitch has clear step-by-step instructions and is accompanied by coloured diagrams. 18 beautiful projects will inspire readers to try out their new skills, with items ranging from bags and accessories to gifts and home decor.
**paperback; 8.25" × 10.75"; 176 pages**
**ISBN-10: 1-44630-166-4**
**ISBN-13: 978-1-44630-166-1**
**SRN: V7939**

### Big Stitch Cross Stitch

Over 30 Contemporary Cross Stitch Projects Using Extra-Large Stitches
Jacqui Pearce
For those who love cross stitch, but lack patience. For those who want fast and fabulous designs to stitch. For those with a larger-than-life love of colorful, hip stitching—this book supersizes it! Using 4, 7 and 10 count canvas, Jacqui Pearce has created a stunning collection of 30 quick-to-complete designs that vary from large projects for the home, to small gifts. This new, fun approach for cross-stitchers taps into the wide range of special XXL lines in manufacturers' collections.
**paperback; 8.5" × 11"; 160 pages**
**ISBN-10: 1-44032-138-8**
**ISBN-13: 978-1-44032-138-2**
**SRN: W8770**

### Stitch Savvy

25 Skill-Building Projects to Take Your Sewing to the Next Level
Deborah Moebes
This book from the author of the best-selling Stitch by Stitch personalizes the instruction by allowing readers to determine their own progression. There are four methods to learning from this book: readers can pick a "track" (Garment Sewing, Bag Making, Home Decor, Patchwork, Sewing for Kids) and work from the tier 1 project all the way to the tier 5. Or, they can just sew what's cutest!
**hardcover; 8" × 10"; 224 pages**
**ISBN-10: 1-44022-947-3**
**ISBN-13: 978-1-44022-947-3**
**SRN: W7260**

These and other fine David & Charles titles are available at your local craft retailer, bookstore or online supplier, or visit our website at **www.mycraftivitystore.com**